POWER AND
INFLUENCE

POWER AND INFLUENCE

John P. Kotter

THE FREE PRESS
A Division of Macmillan, Inc.
NEW YORK

The Free Press
A Division of Macmillan, Inc.
866 Third Avenue, New York, N. Y. 10022

Collier Macmillan Canada, Inc.

Printed in the United States of America

printing number

8 9 10

Library of Congress Cataloging in Publication Data

Kotter, John P.
    Power and influence.

    Bibliography: p.
    Includes index.
    1. Executive ability.   2. Managing your boss.
3. Leadership.   I.   Title.
HD38.2.K68   1985   650.1'3   85–1574
ISBN 0–02–918330–8

Pages 95–114 are adapted from the article "Managing Your Boss" by John J. Gabarro
and John P. Kotter (Harvard Business Review, January–February 1980). Copyright © 1980
by the President and Fellows of Harvard College; all rights reserved.

CONTENTS

PREFACE

This is a book about the causes and the consequences of the increasingly complex social milieu one finds in and around business corporations, law firms, governmental agencies, and other types of organizations which, collectively, employ nearly all of us nowadays. It has been written to draw additional attention to some issues that I think are terribly important and to provide assistance to the many people who are trying to foster excellence, innovation, and responsiveness in their organizations, despite the many forces that promote bureaucracy, parochial politics, and destructive power struggles.

The book's material is presented in four parts. The first, Chapters 1 through 3, lays out the basic argument: that a number of very fundamental economic and social trends have had the cumulative effect over the past few decades of significantly increasing the complexity of the social milieu associated with most managerial, technical, and professional jobs; that this complexity takes the form of complicated interdependent relationships among diverse groups of people; that this increase in diversity and interdependence has converted many individual contributor and management jobs into jobs that demand strong leadership—that is, jobs that require jobholders to get things done through others but do not provide control (in the form of formal authority, budgets, etc.) over all those others; that strong leadership, in this case, means the capacity to develop sufficient sources of power to make up for the power gap inherent in those jobs and the willingness to use that power responsibly to lead the relevant set of subordinates, bosses, peers, and outsiders toward the accomplishment of meaningful goals; and that when such leadership is lacking, as is all too often the case today, the milieu tends to produce conflicts which degenerate into parochial politics, bureaucratic infighting, and destructive power struggles.

In Parts II and III, this leadership challenge is explored more deeply in terms of both high-level executive positions, and lower-level professional and technical jobs. Chapters 4 through 6 describe the day-to-day issues one finds associated with each of the three basic kinds of organizational relationships—those with subordinates, those with superiors, and those with others outside one's chain of command—along with a discussion of what is required to deal with those issues in an effective and responsible manner. Chapters 5 through 7 describe the leadership challenges one often encounters at various stages in a career inside a typical complex organization.

Finally, in Part IV, summary recommendations are offered regarding how one can improve one's personal effectiveness at work, and regarding what needs to be done by our basic institutions if we are to increase significantly over time our supply of people who are capable of handling difficult leadership jobs.

This book has grown out of seven different projects conducted between 1971 and 1983, and supported by the Division of Research at Harvard Business School. A brief description of the projects and the people associated with them can be found in the acknowledgments. Because the results of these projects have been reported in some of my previous books and articles, this book of necessity draws heavily from these sources. Like virtually all of my professional work to date, it is about complex organizations, and it focuses on the behavior of key actors in those organizations. But it is different from earlier work in a few very important ways. It is not a textbook, and although it is based on a considerable amount of research, it is not in any sense a research monograph. Instead, it has been written with the objective of being both as accessible and as helpful as possible to a nonscholarly audience. For that audience, it paints a picture, based on a decade of field research, of some of the central problems and issues created by modern organizations, and of what is required to deal with those issues in organizationally effective, socially responsible, and personally nondestructive ways.

I cannot claim that the book is entirely successful in always walking the narrow line between naïveté and cynicism that it advocates so strongly. Because I do not understand all the nuances of the subjects treated here, I am sure the text occasionally makes either a naïve or a cynical diversion. But for the most part, I think it is on target. I hope, perhaps naïvely, that it can make a small but real difference in some people's lives.

Beyond the yellow brick road of naïveté and the muggers lane of cynicism, there is a narrow path, poorly lit, hard to find, and even harder to stay on once found. People who have the skill and the perseverance to take that path serve us in countless ways. We need more of these people. Many more.

PART I

THE CHANGING NATURE OF MANAGERIAL AND PROFESSIONAL WORK

CHAPTER 1

INTRODUCTION

The basic premise of this book can be stated quite simply: Important changes that are shaping the nature of work in today's complex organizations demand that we become more sophisticated with respect to issues of leadership, power, and influence. With that increased sophistication, we can make our corporations more competitive. We can make rigid bureaucracies more flexible, innovative, and adaptive. We can even make the world of work more exciting and personally satisfying for most people. Without the needed awareness and skill, we risk being overwhelmed by the pathological aspects of modern organizations—the bureaucratic infighting, parochial politics, destructive power struggles, and the like which regularly reduce initiative, innovation, morale, and excellence in all kinds of organizations.

In the pages that follow, I will identify how the nature of professional and managerial work is changing, why it is changing, why leadership and power issues are becoming increasingly important, and what is required to deal with all this in effective and responsible ways. Most of the examples come from corporate settings. They are applicable, however, in governmental agencies, law firms, hospitals—almost everywhere. These examples, along with the interpretations offered, do not provide simple cookbook solutions. But they do offer a way of thinking about subtle yet important issues of relevance to those who work in (or are being trained for) today's complex professional, technical, and managerial jobs. People like Andrea, Fred, and John.

I

Andrea is a 28-year-old copywriter for one of the advertising agencies in New York. She is extremely good at her craft; during the seven years she has been in the advertising business, accounts she has worked for have won six major awards for excellence. Most of the time she loves her work, although it has become increasingly frustrating as she has assumed more responsibility. Most of the time she hates her employer.

It seems hard for Andrea to talk about her work for more than a few minutes without making at least one jab at her firm. She rails against the "idiotic bureaucracy" which limits her capacity to do good work, and she tells amusing stories about two account executives for whom she has rather colorful names. She rarely says anything about her salary, but it is clear she is angry about the size of her raises during the last two years. She harbors a suspicion that one of the "incompetents" in the managerial hierarchy is getting even with her for being outspoken about problems in the firm. The wide-eyed young woman who moved from Ann Arbor to New York seven years ago has traded in her midwestern naïveté for big city cynicism.

Down deep Andrea is worried about her future in the firm. She has considered switching agencies, but her friends tell her it's the same everywhere. When she thinks about conforming and playing "the political game," it makes her want to throw up. She is not sure what other alternatives exist. And that does not make her feel very good. She wishes people would simply leave her alone so she could do the job she loves—an individual contributor's job. Unfortunately, because of the increasing responsibility she has been given over the past few years, she no longer is in such a job.

This book has been written, in part, for the Andreas of the world.

Fred is an up-and-coming young manager in a well-known *Fortune* 500 company. He is thirty-four years old, has an MBA degree, and has been working for his employer for three years. He enjoys his work immensely and has very ambitious plans for the future.

After graduate school, Fred worked for a management consulting firm for five years. Reflecting on those days, Fred says he never had any difficulty with what he calls "the analytics." The real challenges all had to do with people and relationships: learning how to work effectively on a project team; how to interface with clients; how to develop a good reputation with the partners who controlled work assignments; and, eventually, how to manage a project team himself. The problems encountered in these areas were more difficult and complex than he had anticipated. In retrospect, he thinks he was very naïve when he left school.

For the most part, Fred successfully met all the challenges he faced at the consulting firm and was well thought of when he decided to accept an offer of employment from one of his clients. The new job, director of marketing in a manufacturing division with $100 million a year in revenues, was too good to turn down.

Since switching employers, Fred has continued to succeed, but not without great effort on his part. When he arrived at the firm, he encountered considerable hostility directed at the "hotshot MBA consultant." He found that a number of the forty individuals who were a part of his marketing group were not doing an adequate job; but unlike at the consulting firm, he couldn't simply stop using them and substitute other more appropriate staff. In the new job, he has, for the first time, had to deal with an engineering department, two manufacturing plants, and a sales force, departments that often behaved like independent fiefdoms. And also unlike at the consulting firm, his boss and his boss's boss have backgrounds that are very different from his own. These differences often seem to lead them to draw conclusions quite different from his. Convincing them of his point of view has been difficult and frustrating at times.

Fred appreciates that dealing with complex interdependent relationships—with bosses, subordinates, peers, and outsiders—is at the heart of what his managerial job is all about. And he knows he has learned a great deal in this regard since leaving graduate school. But as his fast-track career continuously pushes new and bigger challenges at him, he sometimes gets exhausted trying to keep up with all he needs to know. And he often wishes that he were given more control, more managerial discretion, over the many activities and people for which he is held accountable.

This book has also been written for the Freds of this world.

John is an executive vice president in a West Coast bank. He is forty-four years old, and has been in banking for most of his career. John is proud of his professional accomplishments to date, and wants very much to use his position of responsibility in a meaningful way.

Banking, like many industries today, is going through some interesting changes. John finds these changes both exciting and a little threatening. He has carefully studied the technological trends, changing governmental regulation, and shifting competitive environment; and he thinks he knows what his bank needs to do over the next five years. But he is worried that these things will not be done.

To get from A (where the bank is now) to B (where it needs to be in five years), his firm has to overcome formidable obstacles. First of all, some powerful individuals, departments, and customers must be convinced that there really is a need for the bank to move toward B. Like all change, such movement will require effort, money, and some inconvenience. These people are not yet convinced that they should pay that price. Second, covert opposition from one of the bank's departments that will lose status in a move to B must be overcome. John knows that will not be easy. Third, the chances of one of the three contenders to succeed the current chief executive officer at the bank will probably go down if the bank makes the kinds of changes John is convinced are necessary. Yet that person's cooperation, or at least compliance, is absolutely necessary.

John is sophisticated enough to foresee all these problems, to recognize the potential for a major power struggle at the bank, and to realize that the bank desperately needs strong leadership at this point in its history. He is less sure, however, how he can best influence events in a positive way.

This book is also written for people like John.

II

The fundamental purpose of this book is to help people like Andrea, Fred, and John to be more effective in their jobs, and more successful in their careers—and then, through them, to help make their organizations more competitive, responsive, and responsible. The focus of this effort is on a wide variety of leadership, power, and influence issues—issues that have been gaining increasing importance in the past few decades. Such issues include:

- How to implement important strategic or adaptive change, despite the need for many people's cooperation in the effort, and despite the fact that some of those people are strongly inclined to resist cooperating.
- How to foster entrepreneurial and creative behavior inside a firm, despite dozens of bureaucratic obstacles that are difficult or impossible to remove.
- How to gain the resources, support, and fair treatment from bosses (even less than completely competent bosses) that one needs to perform a difficult job without succumbing to cheap (and organizationally harmful) political games.
- How to avoid developing destructive adversarial relationships with people whose help and cooperation you absolutely need, but who are outside your chain of command (and your direct control) and who tend to be suspicious of you.

- How to get subordinates to work together as a team for the greater good, instead of succumbing to the natural tendency to fight with each other and become turf-oriented.
- How to avoid becoming a casualty in a corporate power struggle, especially when you are fairly young, weak, and vulnerable.
- How to avoid falling into one of the many traps which lead to power misuse—such as not grooming a successor and not turning over the reins of power at the appropriate time.
- In general, how to foster excellence, innovation, and responsiveness and not get bogged down in bureaucracy, parochial politics, or unproductive power struggles.

People do exist who are able to deal with these issues very effectively. You will see some of these individuals used as examples later in the book. But such people are in the minority today. And that is a problem of some significance, because these issues have become enormously important. In my opinion, they will become even more important in the decades to come.

I didn't always think this way. When I first began doing field research and consulting in organizations, I had a very different conception of what the key issues were. Fifteen years ago, I thought the reason many organizations performed poorly was because they lacked "good" or "modern" ideas about products, markets, market research, control systems, strategic planning, inventory control, etc. I had just learned these "ideas" in graduate school and was all excited about spreading the word to the uneducated masses.

I quickly discovered two things, especially through my consulting:

1. Good ideas are rarely lacking inside even poorly performing firms. As a consultant, all I needed to do was go around and interview enough people, summarize the better ideas, and voilà! I would have a first-class report bursting with excellent recommendations.
2. Having a good idea is one thing, implementing it is

something else again. The reason firms have excellent ideas in them, and yet still perform poorly, is that the people who have the ideas can't get them implemented. Bureaucratic and political obstacles stifle their creativity and innovation.

After studying this problem for over a decade now, I think I understand why it is that some people are incredibly effective at providing leadership in getting things done inside complex organizations, while most of us are not. It begins with a certain way of thinking about the social milieu in which one operates. This way of thinking about what "work" means is different from that held by many of us, especially with regard to issues of power, dependence, and influence.

Most of us, to be blunt, are remarkably naïve when it comes to understanding power dynamics in complex organizations. At the same time, others of us are incredibly cynical. Ironically, although the cynics and the naïves see themselves as almost opposites in outlook, when it comes to performance in today's managerial and professional jobs, they have very similar problems. Both distort social reality and thus act on bad information, which inevitably produces problems for them. The naïves distort reality by viewing it through rose-colored glasses, the cynics look through charcoal-colored protective eyewear.

A couple of years ago I tried an experiment with some of our MBA students to see just how naive or how cynical these very bright and capable young people were. I gave a group of about one hundred of them a five-page description of a business situation in which some major changes were needed. They were given two hours to analyze the situation and write a set of basic (not detailed) recommendations for a particular manager. I then had their responses coded for naïveté and cynicism. The procedure used was straightforward. Whenever someone drew a conclusion or made a recommendation based on an unstated assumption—one not justified by the data in the five-page description—that certain people had unselfish motives, or that people had warm and supportive relationships, or that people always wanted to cooperate with each other, the response was given one point for naïveté.

Conversely, whenever someone made an unjustified assumption about people having selfish motives, about the existence of adversarial relationships, about the inevitability of conflict among people, or the like, the response was given one point for cynicism. These points were then added up, and each student's paper was put into one of six categories: very naïve, somewhat naïve, somewhat cynical, very cynical, neither, or very mixed.

Think for a moment. What would you expect the results to be? These people ranged in age from twenty-three to thirty-six. They were all very well educated. Nearly 90 percent had had some full-time business experience. What do you think?

The results:

Naïve	46%
Cynical	18%
Neither	31%
Very mixed	5%

I will have more to say later in the book about why very capable twenty-six-year-olds, like those that participated in the experiment, seem to be so naïve (and why some are cynical). Basically it has to do with the kinds of situations they have been exposed to—situations almost entirely in educational organizations and in their nuclear families.

I have never been able to do as systematic an experiment with an older group of managers. But my impression is that, among those who are most effective, both the "naïve" and the "cynical" percentages would be *much* lower. (For ineffective older managers, I suspect both the "naïve" and the "neither" percentages would be somewhat lower, and that the cynical percentage would be much higher.) My sense is that really effective managers and professionals were pretty naïve when they were twenty-six, much like my students. But they gave up their naïveté during the early stages of their careers for a more complex, sophisticated, and realistic vision of the social reality around them. Ineffective older managers simply traded naïve views for cynical ones.

It is also my impression that the process by which effective organizational leaders learn more sophisticated approaches to their work begins with exposure to those approaches, as well as exposure to the pitfalls of more naïve or cynical methods. And that, in a nutshell, is what much of this book will attempt to provide.

III

It is naïve to assume that any book by itself can completely reorient a person's way of handling social reality, especially since reading does not necessarily build social skills. But reading can give us new ways of thinking. It can refocus our attention on more important issues and problems. It can help us to reorder our agenda for our own professional development. In these ways, it can help us to help ourselves become more effective at work.

Competent and responsible performance in managerial and professional jobs inside complex organizations is more important today than ever before. At no other time in history has mankind been more dependent on corporations, governments, hospitals, schools, and other organizations. The thousands of goods and services we use, and often take for granted, almost all come from organizations managed by professionals and managers. The very quality of our lives and our environment today is largely determined by these organizations.

Organizational excellence is impossible without individual excellence. And individual excellence today, especially in managerial and professional jobs, demands much more than technical competence. It demands a sophisticated type of social skill: a leadership skill that can mobilize people and accomplish important objectives despite dozens of obstacles; a skill that can pull people together for meaningful purposes despite the thousands of forces that push us apart; a skill that can keep our important corporations and public institutions from descending into a mediocrity characterized by bureaucratic infighting, parochial politics, and vicious power struggles.

Managerial and professional excellence requires the knack of knowing how to make power dynamics in corporate life work for us, instead of against us.

CHAPTER 2

DIVERSITY, INTERDEPENDENCE, AND POWER DYNAMICS IN ORGANIZATIONS
Beyond Naïveté and Cynicism

I have in front of me a stack of books that is nearly as tall as I am. These are textbooks on finance, accounting, decision analysis, management, statistics for business, economics, marketing, organizational behavior, operations research, management information systems, business policy, and personnel. Some of these books are used in undergraduate education, some in MBA programs, and some in executive education. These books, and the instructors that use them, influence hundreds of thousands of people each year.

I have just gone through the table of contents and index of each of these books looking for terms like *power struggle, parochial politics,* and *bureaucratic infighting.* Thousands of topics are covered in these books. But not those topics. There are only a few pages that come close to addressing them explicitly. A few pages out of a total of about 19,000.

The picture of life in business and other types of organizations that one gets from these books is one in which people use sophisticated analytical tools to make decisions about pricing, inventory level, resource allocation, debt limit, incentive compensation, and other business matters. Getting the information needed to use these tools does not seem to be a problem. Nor does implementing the decisions. It is a picture almost devoid of conflict, struggle, manipulation, antagonism, fighting, and the like. It is a very naïve picture.

I

Between 1950 and 1970, sales at Johns-Manville, Inc. grew at an average annual rate of about 4 percent. The company had developed a reputation as "stodgy, starchy, and sleepy." [1] Insiders say that the firm had no real strategy at all. One company veteran had been quoted as saying that they "kept the plants running and hoped for the best."

In 1969, aware that at least two other firms were contemplating acquiring the company, its directors demanded that Clinton Burnett, the president, do something "to rejuvenate Johns-Manville and give it the strength to survive." One of the ways in which Burnett responded was by hiring Richard Goodwin, a consultant, as vice president of planning. Twenty months later, the board was sufficiently impressed by Goodwin that they moved Burnett up to chairman and made Goodwin president and chief executive officer.

Between 1970 and 1975, Goodwin did nothing less than, in *Fortune's* words, "rejuvenate the once torpid building materials company." He reorganized, made eleven major acquisitions and twelve divestitures, moved the company's headquarters from New York to Denver, and introduced a new style of management. Sales responded by leaping from $578 million in 1970 to $1.1 billion in 1975, an increase of 91 percent. Between 1970 and 1974, net income went up 115 percent.

Despite these results, Goodwin's somewhat flamboyant and independent style (he wore modishly long hair and played a hot jazz piano) is said to have irked the conservative outside directors. In 1976, two of Goodwin's specific proposals created additional friction. In the first, Goodwin requested that Johns-Manville change one of its oldest financial ties. In the second, he proposed that the number of directors be increased from twelve to fifteen and later to twenty.

In September 1976, after arriving in New York for a board meeting, Goodwin was asked by three of the outside directors for a brief discussion in his hotel suite. The three directors told Goodwin that they represented all nine outside directors on Johns-Manville's twelve-person board and that they wanted him to resign. Goodwin demanded to know why. "Under the bylaws of this corporation," he was told, "we don't have to give you a reason." Two hours later, the three directors were gone, taking with them a signed separation agreement, and leaving a stunned former chief executive officer.

Jones, Day, Reaves, and Pogue was the sixth largest law firm in the country, with headquarters in Cleveland and branches in Washington and Los Angeles. It was an old and prestigious firm with 220 lawyers. Its partners included a former Harvard Law School dean, a former secretary of HUD, one of the Ohio Tafts, and a former undersecretary of the Treasury. Many people thought of the firm as the best and most solid legal group west of the Hudson.[2]

The Washington office of Jones, Day was headed by Welch Pogue. Nearly eighty years old, Pogue was near the end of a very distinguished career as a lawyer and law firm manager. He took great pride in the fact that the office he helped build was very successful and the fact that his son was scheduled to take over the management of the entire firm in a few years.

During the first half of 1979, a power struggle erupted within Jones, Day, a struggle that centered around the Washington office and Welch Pogue. Many of the details surrounding this struggle are not public, but this much is known: In a meeting on January 15, 1979, with Elden Crowell, the head of the firm's government contracts department, Pogue announced that it would be in the best interests of the firm for Crowell and three other government contracts partners to leave. Pogue did not explain, at least to Crowell's satisfaction, why the four lawyers should go. And in any event, Crowell was not at all inclined just to pack up his law books and move out.

Almost immediately after this fateful meeting, Crowell began to mobilize support against the decision. He was particularly successful with some of the younger Washington partners, who decided to see if they could reverse the decision by electing a new managing partner. The firm's partnership agreement stated that if holders of two-thirds of the ownership shares in the Washington office voted to change the office's management, their vote would be binding. After a short but intense round of lobbying, they succeeded in getting the needed two-thirds vote. And on January 26, Pogue resigned as managing partner.

On February 14, the new management of the Washington office met with the Cleveland managing partner, Allen Holmes, at the Metropolitan Club in Washington. At that meeting, Holmes announced his support for Pogue's original decision and stated that he would ask the entire partnership for a vote regarding the government contracts partners. He did so knowing the Cleveland and Los Angeles partners would stand behind him.

By the time the dust finally settled on this affair six months later, two-thirds of the Washington office had decided to leave and establish a new law firm. In the course of this upheaval, incalculable hours of valuable professional time had been spent talking, lobbying, calculating, scheming, arguing, and negotiating. And a very proud man named Pogue was left wondering why his extremely distinguished career was ending this way.

On Thursday, August 21, 1980, at 6:13 P.M., ABC's *World News Tonight* ran a four-and-a-half-minute segment detailing allegations of criminal fraud, conspiracy, and conflict of interest against a number of executives in a large United States corporation. The fact that a network news program would run an expose on an organization or its leaders surprised no one. But the news report was, nevertheless, news in itself, because the corporation involved was ABC, Inc.[3]

The so-called *Charlie's Angels* scandal was uncovered originally by the *New York Times*. ABC News subsequently investigated it in more depth, turning up additional damaging information. The overall accusations made against ABC, Inc. basically boiled down to this: (1) that executives at ABC were involved in a scheme to defraud the "profit participants" in *Charlie's Angels* of close to $1 million, diverting a large part of that money to Spelling-Goldberg Productions via "creative accounting"; (2) that a lawyer in ABC's West Coast contracts division was fired when she tried to bring this to the attention of ABC executives; and (3) that a very close friend of Aaron Spelling and Leonard Goldberg, a friend whose children all worked for either Spelling or Goldberg and who was a partner in some real estate deals, was none other than Elton Rule, the president of ABC.

In November 1980, *Fortune* ran a follow-up article on the story, adding one new dimension not in the *ABC News* report. It seems that ABC's chairman, then seventy-four years old, was expected to retire sometime soon. Rule was his most likely replacement. Among other top executives, the most aggressively ambitious was believed to be Roone Arledge. Arledge and Rule were, in the words of one ABC employee, "about as friendly as Iran and Iraq." Roone Arledge was in charge of *ABC News.*

II

When confronted with situations such as Goodwin's dismissal, the "split" at Jones, Day, or the "scandal" at ABC, the naïve among us are shocked, while the cynical chuckle knowingly. The former would like us to believe that these stories are aberrations or possibly not even true (perhaps the product of a cynical journalist's imagination). The latter feel that this is what daily life in organizations is all about and that the only reason we do not hear of these stories constantly is because they are suppressed by people who have a stake in not letting the truth be known.

The reality is that these stories are not the result of a cynical journalist's imagination. The facts, for the most part, are verifiable. Dozens of similar episodes have been reported over the last few decades, both by journalists and by those applied social scientists who specialize in organization studies.[4] A naïve perspective simply does not fit the facts.

But at the same time, a cynical perspective does not offer a much more useful explanation. On the surface, at least, these kinds of stories are not inconsistent with a cynic's view of the world. But a cynical perspective is unable to explain or predict where and when episodes like these will be found, and where and when they will not. Cynics expect destructive power struggles, bureaucratic infighting, and parochial politics to be almost everywhere almost all the time. But facts do not support such a conclusion. Best evidence suggests that although pathological power processes are found, to some degree, in almost all organizations, some firms—usually the best performing ones—are remarkably free of such processes.

The problem with the cynical perspective is that it *assumes* firms like Jones, Day blow apart, organizations like ABC are plagued by scandal, and executives like Dick Goodwin are fired because of the essence of human nature, which they believe is dark, competitive, self-centered, and fundamentally immoral. The cynic, much like the naïve (ironically), attributes organizational outcomes to forces inside individuals—the cynic assumes evil forces are usually at work, the naïve assumes good forces are the norm. At the same time, both are almost blind to the social milieu surrounding people inside organizations and how that milieu can shape behavior, systematically create conflicts among people, and set the stage for the kinds of power struggles described at the beginning of the chapter.[5]

An alternative perspective—one that emphasizes the impact of the complex social milieu—will be used in this book. Such a perspective employs two basic concepts: diversity and interdependence. Diversity, as I shall use the term, refers to differences among people with respect to goals, values, stakes, assumptions, and perceptions. Interdependence refers to a state in which two or more parties have power over each other because they are, to some degree, dependent on each other. This can be contrasted with a state of independence, where parties have no power over each other (are not dependent on each other) and with a state of unilateral dependence (or dominance) where one party has considerable power over another, but not vice versa.

The logic of how high levels of diversity and interdependence set the stage for the kinds of interactions seen in the cases described above can be summarized as follows:

First of all, when a high degree of interdependence exists in the workplace, unilateral action is rarely possible. For all decisions of any significance, many people will be in a position to retard, block, or sabotage action, because they have some power over the situation. This power might be based on the formal authority of their positions, on financial or human resources they control, on their special expertise or knowledge, on legislation or legal contracts, or on any number of other things.

When the many parties who are linked together interdependently are very diverse from one another, they will naturally have difficulty agreeing on what should be done, who should do it, and when. Differences in goals, values, stakes, and outlook will lead different people to different conclusions. The greater the diversity, and the greater the interdependence, the more differences of opinion there will be. Because of the interdependence, people will not be able to resolve these differences either by edict or by walking away. As a result, high levels of diversity and interdependence in the workplace are quite naturally linked to conflicting opinions about action and thereby influence attempts to resolve that conflict.

When few people are involved (a very limited amount of interdependence), and when differences among those people are small (very limited diversity), resolving conflicts at work in both efficient and effective ways is a fairly simple procedure. The parties can get together, confront the issues in a straightforward way, and search for a creative solution that satisfies the key needs of all the people involved. Or they can defer to the person who has the most relevant knowledge or expertise, who will then search for the optimum solution and, once he has it, present it to the others. When there are a lot of people involved (lots of interdependence), and when the differences among the people are great (a high level of diversity), resolving conflicts in efficient and effective ways becomes much more difficult and complex. It is one thing to resolve a conflict with a fellow marketing employee who works in the same location and for the same division of a firm as you do and who has an educational and ethnic background similar to your own. It is quite a different case if the other person is an engineer (or an accountant) who was born and lives in another country, works for another division, etc. And it is a completely different case if the person is a government employee (or a member of the press) who thinks of you as "the enemy."

Under conditions of high diversity and interdependence, the people involved will rarely agree on a single "expert" to whom they can defer. Different groups will propose different experts. Getting all the relevant parties together to discuss the issue usually becomes impractical. If representatives of the key constituencies get together, great differences in outlook make discussion difficult, time consuming, and frustrating. Under those circumstances, people typically begin looking for other ways to resolve the conflict. Sometimes they will try to negotiate a nonoptimum compromise. Or they will try to force their opinion on others. Or they will allow the other parties to make the decision, with the implicit expectation that, in the future, those others will return the favor. Or they will try to manipulate the other parties into accepting their point of view. Or they will try to persuade others that their solution is really best for everyone. Any of those tactics can, under the right circumstance, resolve a conflict. But they often do so at a considerable price. Forcing a solution on others invites retaliation in the future. A compromise is by definition not an optimum solution. Persuasion often takes a lot of time and effort. Manipulation can lead to a loss of trust among people, making conflict resolution more difficult in the future. And, when the level of diversity and interdependence is great enough, these tactics can simply fail, leading to a protracted power struggle, characterized by bureaucratic infighting and parochial politics.

In other words, under conditions of great diversity and interdependence, the potential automatically exists for the types of episodes seen in the Manville; Jones, Day; and ABC cases, quite independent of the inherent goodness or badness of the people involved. Large differences in goals, perspective, stakes, and outlook between a very interdependent chief executive officer and his board of directors can create the potential for the conflicts that emerged in the Johns-Manville case. Equally large cultural and business differences between economically interdependent branch offices of a law firm can produce the kinds of conflicts seen in the Jones, Day case. Likewise, large differences in outlook between the business and creative sides of a television network, along with the competing interests of potential rivals at that network, can easily produce the basis for the kinds of problems seen in the ABC case. In all these situations, and in hundreds of others that are fundamentally similar, social complexity, not character, is the key driving force. And when such situations are not handled with great skill—a leadership skill that was somewhat lacking in all three of those cases—destructive power struggles are almost inevitable. (This is summarized in Figure 2–1.)

In a similar manner, a social complexity perspective would predict that under conditions of low diversity and interdependence one would tend to find little conflict along with few power struggles, little bureaucratic infighting, and little if any parochial politics. Such conditions might be associated with:

- Small size—where one usually finds little job specialization.
- Technological simplicity—where lots of different kinds of technological experts are not needed.
- Little product or service diversification—where everyone is focused on the same business objectives.
- Little competition—where resources are abundant and people don't have to coordinate all their actions closely with everyone else, or where customers and suppliers have relatively little power.
- Lots of small customers and suppliers—where none is big enough to have any real power.

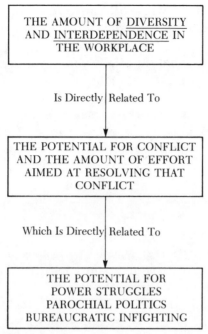

FIGURE 2-1

- Little if any government regulation—where governmental units have little power.
- Few if any unions—where organized employee groups have little power.
- A homogeneous work force—where few differences exist in sex, age, nationality, race, etc.
- A poorly educated work force—where no one has power based on special expertise.

A social complexity perspective would argue that it is not by chance that the economists' traditional model of a firm, where only "rational" economic decision making occurred, and where power struggles and politics were nonexistent, was a small and technologically simple organization that operated in an environment without large customers, suppliers, unions, or governmental regulators, and that employed a relatively homogeneous labor force in a simple organization structure.

If we lived in a world dominated by organizations that look like the economists' traditional model of the firm, the discussion in this chapter would be interesting, but irrelevant. Such a world of social simplicity did exist—indeed, it existed for most of human history, including that period when traditional economic theory was first developed. But that has changed in the last century, especially in the last few decades. Today, we no longer have a socially simple world. And powerful forces are making it more, rather than less, complex all the time.

III

I think we often forget how much has changed in the past one hundred years. The world of work for a typical person before 1840 was a struggle against nature. That person, and most of his forebears during the preceding 10,000 years, was a poor farmer. He spent most of his time working with things, not with people. There were some work-related interdependent relationships—perhaps between the farmer and the owner of the closest general store—but not many. And those people who did depend on one another tended not to be a very diverse lot; they often had similar educational, religious, ethnic, and national backgrounds. Conflicts among these parties certainly existed from time to time, but they were few in number and relatively straightforward in content. Work energy went mainly into plowing, seeding, mending, feeding, etc.

Of course executives in 1840 and before faced a considerably more complex milieu. But there were not that many executives back then; those helping to run organizations employing 500 or more people numbered in the hundreds (or a few thousand at most) in 1840, versus over a million today. And for most of these early executives the number of important interdependent relationships and the diversity of the people in those relationships were very small compared to what they are today.

An executive in 1840 would typically have to deal with a

very limited geographical market. Transportation and communication difficulties made serving a larger market either impossible or uneconomical. He probably would have had to depend on a few local suppliers, but not many. Products and services were technologically simple and did not require a significant number of different inputs. Some form of government could not be ignored, but it was undoubtedly small and limited in its demands. Inside the organization, the executive would have been somewhat dependent on key employees, but there would have been very few of them. Relatively uncomplicated technology, simple products, and a small volume required a small number of simple jobs which could be staffed by easily replaceable people. And the employee group would have been relatively homogeneous overall, drawn from a relatively homogeneous local labor pool.

A typical executive today works in a completely different world. A century and a half of technological evolution has produced communication and transportation technologies which make our entire planet a global marketplace. Medical, agricultural, and other industrial technological advances have increased the population in that market dramatically and have given most a vastly increased purchasing power. Industrial technologies, beginning with the steam engine, have led to larger and larger factories to produce products for that marketplace. As industrial and retail organizations grew in size and number, more and more organizations of a different sort emerged either to provide services for these firms (e.g., accounting firms) or to regulate their behavior (e.g., the Federal Trade Commission, the United Auto Workers) or to provide services for their increasingly urbanized factory-oriented labor force (e.g., schools, hospitals, local government).

As a result of the changes brought about by technology, a typical executive today has to deal with thousands of interdependent relationships—linkages to people, groups, or organizations that have the power to affect his job performance. And the diversity of goals, opinions, and beliefs among these players is typically enormous.[6]

It is not unusual for an executive today, even in a relatively small company, to have to deal with hundreds of different markets in dozens of countries. He or she might serve these markets with 20, 200, or even 2,000 different technologically complex products or services, all of which demand a huge network of suppliers for parts, people, and money. In addition, there might be any number of unions, government units, even media organizations that are relevant and important and powerful. Inside the firm this person will be dependent on a highly specialized labor force organized into subunits that have different missions. The labor force will typically include both young and old, black and white, men and women, MBAs and high school dropouts, U.S. citizens and others. And many of these people will work in complex jobs where they cannot be replaced quickly and easily.

Although this social complexity peaks in executive jobs, it is found to some degree today in almost all managerial, professional, and technical work. Particularly since World War II, the growth of increasingly complex organizations has forced executives to decentralize, which means asking more and more middle level managers and professionals to help deal with some of the diversity and interdependence. And dozens of different trends have increased either diversity or interdependence at almost all levels during the past twenty-five years. These trends include:

1. The internationalization of business: A typical business today operates in more countries, gets much more revenue from outside the United States, and competes against more non-U.S. firms than did its counterpart twenty years ago.
2. Growth through diversification: Most firms today are much larger than they were in 1960, and much of that growth has come through diversification—that is, through the addition of new products or services or market areas.
3. The growth of government regulation, organized consumer groups, and the business press: Today, unlike twenty years ago, there are many more entities besides

customers, suppliers, competitors, and unions that attempt to influence the behavior of business firms.

4. An increasingly heterogeneous work force: With the influx of large numbers of women, Blacks, Spanish-speaking Browns, and other minorities, the work force is no longer a relatively homogeneous pool of white males.
5. Continuing technological advances: New microprocessor technologies, genetic technologies, and other advances have erected whole new industries and helped reshape old ones.
6. An increasingly educated work force: This is certainly not a new trend, but it is one that continues to change the social milieu of the workplace in important ways.
7. The slowdown in the world economy in the last decade: This is perhaps the newest of all the trends and the one that many businesses feel most intensely.
8. The aging of the work force: World War II baby-boomers are now working, and their large numbers have greatly intensified the competition for a limited number of places in corporate hierarchies.

Experts might argue about which of these trends is more important and about whether I have left an item or two off the list. But I don't think they would disagree with two points: (1) these are *real* trends and (2) they each are having an impact of some importance on the world of work. Although a considerable amount has been written about the effect of each of these trends individually, virtually nothing has been written about their cumulative impact on professional and managerial work. It is this cumulative effect which is interesting and important for our purposes here.

By taking away autonomy and discretion and by making the jobs more and more dependent on others, a number of these trends have been systematically turning individual-contributor jobs (positions in which all the critical tasks associated with the job responsibilities can be performed by the individual holding the job) and management jobs (jobs that require the incumbent to get tasks done through others, but at the same time give that person considerable power over those key others) into leadership jobs (positions that require a person to get others to help and cooperate but, unlike management jobs, do not give the job holder control over most of those key others). Such trends include (1) the growth in the power of nonmarket third parties, such as the government, consumer groups, the media, and, in certain industries, organized labor; (2) the growth of international competition, which has made U.S. firms more dependent on important customers and suppliers, and by reducing their margins and profitability, has made their internal departments and divisions more dependent on each other for limited resources; (3) the growth of increasingly sophisticated technologies—both managerial and physical science technologies—which have made us more and more dependent on staff who specialize in those technologies; and (4) the growth of an increasingly educated and technically competent work force—a work force that cannot be ordered about or as easily replaced as their predecessors.

Taken together, these trends have in the past twenty to thirty years significantly changed many managerial and individual contributor jobs. And they will continue to change those jobs. These trends are making people more and more dependent on government officials, technical experts, key subordinates, other departments in their firms, key customers, important suppliers, major unions, the business press, and so forth without automatically giving them additional ways to control these groups. As a result, they are turning individual contributor and management jobs into leadership jobs—jobs in which there is a sizeable built-in gap between the power one needs to get the job done well and the power that automatically comes with the job.

At the same time, a number of other trends have made these emerging leadership jobs increasingly complex by making the people that have to be led a more and more diverse group of others—trends like product diversification, market diversification, and the increasing heterogeneity of the work force.

There was a time not long ago when the typical manager or professional in a U.S. corporation dealt with only a single product or service, a single market or set of customers, and a work force that was a mirror image of himself. No longer. Today we often have to deal with multiple products or services, which demand that we work with people who have different business objectives and perspectives. We often have to deal with multiple markets and customer groups, people who have different needs and who sometimes even speak different languages. We have to work with fellow employees who are no longer just like us—indeed, who are sometimes very different.

This recent increase in the diversity of the people with whom we must interact at work has profound implications. It is one thing to lead a group of people who are all pretty much like yourself in background, training, and outlook. It is quite a different case if those others are focusing on a variety of different products and markets, and if they are black and white, young and old, American and Asian. Diversity among interdependent parties produces conflict, often a lot of conflict, which can be very difficult to resolve in a productive way. Resolving conflicts in a productive way that pulls people together, instead of driving them farther apart, and which produces creative decisions, instead of destructive power struggles, is a high-level leadership skill.

In other words, a number of fundamental trends of our times have been turning jobs that once looked like this:

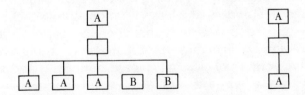

where associated with each job there were a limited number of clearly identified relationships to a relatively homogeneous group of people, into complex leadership jobs that look more like this:

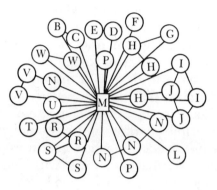

where there are many interdependent relationships, sometimes not clearly identified, to a very diverse group of people.

With this great increase in social complexity has come a corresponding (and predictable) increase in conflict among people at work and in the effort spent trying to overcome this conflict. Decreasing autonomy has forced people to allocate more and more time seeking to get others to help or to cooperate or to comply with their decisions. But increased diversity has made this a more and more difficult task. A decision about a new product specification that satisfies the engineers in a firm is often unacceptable to the marketing people. A delivery-time decision that satisfies one customer often has unacceptable consequences for another customer or for certain manufacturing managers. A policy decision that satisfies one set of government regulators is often unacceptable to those managers who must carry out the policy and is sometimes unacceptable to yet another set of government regulators. Wage decisions that please a union upset stockholders. Resource-allocation decisions that increase capital spending in one division of a firm may upset managers in other divisions. Affirmative-action policies that please minorities and women displease many white males. A new product design that pleases customers in Germany may be unacceptable to customers in Brazil.

The sheer magnitude of all of this conflict is staggering. Each and every day millions of conflicts emerge, sometimes over the most trivial issues (where to put the water cooler), and sometimes over issues of monumental importance (nuclear arms). In complex organizations today, it is a rare decision issue or implementation issue that is devoid of at least the potential for conflict.

In other words, the potential for the kind of situations seen in the Manville; Jones, Day; and ABC cases has increased dramatically in the past century, with most of the change coming in the last two decades. This shift has not occurred because human nature has suddenly become much more self-centered, competitive, and evil, but because a number of major trends have made the social milieu at work much more complex. And there is no evidence that those trends will all reverse themselves anytime in the foreseeable future.

IV

It is almost impossible to overstate the significance of the changing nature of managerial and professional work. The stakes associated with our finding intelligent ways to adapt to these changes are huge.

Hundreds of large organizations, and thousands of small ones, face the potential problems encountered in the Manville; Jones, Day; and ABC examples. How well they deal with these challenges affects millions of customers, employees, stockholders and others.

Take the case of AT&T for example. Deregulation has made the new AT&T less dependent on the government. But powerful new competition and changing technologies have vastly increased its dependence on customers and competitors, which in turn has greatly increased internal interdependence, especially among its engineering, production, and marketing personnel. No longer can the various functions operate fairly autonomously, while manufacturing calls the key shots in order to keep costs down and to keep the government happy. Now innovation and speed to market are key. This requires that manufacturing no longer dominates decisions, and that all the key functions work much more closely together.

How well AT&T is able to manage this new internal inter-dependence will affect the quality of service it offers to its millions of customers. It will affect the job security and job satisfaction of its hundreds of thousands of employees. It will affect the financial returns offered its millions of stockholders.

How well is AT&T meeting this challenge so far? According to many reports, not particularly well.[7] Manufacturing and marketing executives seem to be locked in a major power struggle which is draining energy away from the real tasks at hand. And evidence, as of this writing, suggests that the manufacturing camp is currently winning the battle; between September 1983 and February 1984 three of AT&T's most senior marketing executives left the company (along with others below them). One somewhat bitter former marketing manager has been quoted as summarizing the situation this way:

> I left ATT because the market-driven organization we were trying to achieve was losing out to the manufacturing mentality. The marketers want to supply the customer with what they need quickly, while the manufacturers want to take more time to make a product that is twice as expensive with half the options. It's a clash in corporate culture that produces battle after battle between these two segments. I'm relieved to be out of all the political turmoil.

The people running AT&T are not so dumb or naïve as not to recognize that strong responsible leadership is needed throughout the organization to help pull it through this diffi-cult transition. But so far they have not been entirely success-ful in finding, developing, or encouraging enough of that leadership.

Is this situation unique? After talking to hundreds of execu-tives in dozens of U.S. organizations, I don't think so. The challenge at AT&T is bigger and more visible than the chal-lenge at many other firms. But the roots of the problems are similar.

In a world of great diversity and interdependence in the workplace, strong leadership is needed throughout organiza-tions to manage that complex social milieu. And when it is not forthcoming, the consequences are very serious indeed.

CHAPTER 3

THE LEADERSHIP
CHALLENGE
Making Social Complexity Work
for Us, Not Against Us

The analysis presented in the previous chapter can be summarized as follows: The work organizations which dominate our world today, and which will probably play an even greater role in the foreseeable future, have characteristics that often create a large and incredibly complex set of interdependent relationships among highly diverse groups of people, some of whom may be spread out across nations or continents. Considerable diversity among people who are interdependent in complex ways inevitably leads to conflicts and attempts to influence events. The interdependence forces people, at least to some minimum degree, to interact with others. The diversity often makes it difficult during those interactions to agree on who should do what. Hence, conflict emerges. Again, because of interdependence, people cannot simply ignore the conflict. They are forced to try to influence events so as to try to resolve it. But because of differences in goals, priorities, and beliefs, resolving the conflict in a mutually satisfactory way can be difficult, time-consuming, and frustrating. So people sometimes stop trying to find a mutually satisfactory decision and look for ways to win for themselves. And that, in turn, easily evolves into parochial political processes and destructive power struggles. And with these pathological power processes often comes even more diversity, the product of adversarial attitudes, and more interdependence, the result of political games, all of which creates even more conflict and an increasingly difficult situation to manage.[1]

Dealing with this pathology is truly one of the great challenges of our times.

I

The potential for the kinds of problems described in Chapter 2 is not evenly distributed across the landscape. The greater the scope and diversity of an organization's activities, the more sophisticated the technologies it employs, the more competitive or resource-poor its environment, the larger the other organizations in its environment, the more diverse its labor force in training and culture and age, the more specialized the positions in its structure, and the larger the management hierarchy, the greater will be the diversity and interdependence, and the greater will be the potential for conflict and power struggles and politics. This means we would normally expect to find more complicated influence processes, politics, and power struggles in certain settings than in others. But even in two organizations that are identical in the characteristics mentioned above, the consequences of these characteristics can be very different depending upon the skills and attitudes of people in leadership jobs. And this is the key point: Great diversity and interdependence does not inevitably lead to destructive situations. Quite the contrary, that kind of social milieu can produce excellent decisions, highly creative solutions, and very innovative products and services, if it is handled in an effective and responsible way.

People who have studied decision-making processes have often observed that diversity and interdependence are essential ingredients in fostering original ideas. If there is only one person involved in a decision-making situation (no interdependencies), or if the group of individuals involved all think pretty much the same way (no diversity), the breadth of information brought to bear on a problem is almost always narrow in scope. When a number of people are involved, and when they have different perspectives, more information gets into the process often because more conflict develops. The conflict forces people to stop and think and look for ways to resolve it.

The "Desert Survival Situation," an exercise often used in group decision-making courses and seminars, demonstrates this tendency well. In this exercise, participants are given only a few pages of information about a group of people who have crash landed in a desert in the southwestern United States. They are told what resources these "survivors" have at their disposal (fifteen items) and are asked to rank these items in order of their importance to the survival of the people involved. After all the participants have made their decisions individually, they are put into small groups and asked to reach a consensus. As it turns out, the group decision is better than the average of the individual decisions in more than four out of five cases. And when the participants are skilled at handling this kind of situation, the group decision is often better than the decision made by any of the individuals involved.

People who have studied organizations have made very similar observations. Corporations that are leaders in their industries and those that help start new industries tend to be full of diversity, interdependence, and conflict, often by explicit design. The people running these firms sometimes purposely create seemingly messy organizational structures, full of complex interdependent relationships. They encourage and even force diverse elements to interact. In doing so, they realize that more conflicts will then emerge and that this can create more short-term problems and challenges. But they also realize that if those conflicts can be productively managed, the result will be more original thinking, more creative solutions to business problems, and more innovative products and services. And they have learned that such originality can make them more competitive, responsive, and adaptive.

Take new product development, for example. Leading corporations often involve engineers and marketers and manufac-

turers—and sometimes customers, suppliers, and still others—
in the development process, even though they realize that
this will make the process more difficult to manage, because
it will generate a lot of conflict. They do so because they
recognize that the alternative, leaving product development
to the engineers or to the marketers alone, usually produces
an inferior product, although the process itself is easier to
manage. Products developed by engineers alone tend to be
technologically sophisticated, and state-of-the-art. But they are
often difficult to manufacture, and they often do not meet a
real market need—at least at a price consumers are willing
to pay. Products developed by marketers alone are usually
responsive to today's real market demand, but they are just
as often technologically infeasible or will soon be technologically obsolescent. Similarly, new products developed by manufacturing people tend to be easy to manufacture, and hence
often inexpensive. But they are usually unresponsive to shifting market demand and technological change.

All of the great corporations with which I have worked—
the IBMs and GEs of the world—recognize these realities.[2]
They don't hire a homogeneous group of organization men
and put them in relatively autonomous jobs in a structured
hierarchy, although it is tempting to do so when the frustration
of managing great social complexity gets high. Instead, they
accept that some social complexity and conflict are inevitable,
and they actively try to manage it. And when they are successful, the very process of managing conflict productively pulls
people together, eliminating unnecessary differences and po-
litically inspired interdependencies. That, in turn, reduces unproductive conflict and makes the process of managing social
complexity more feasible.

The ailing firms with which I have worked have usually
taken a very different path. In these firms, one typically finds
that, in order to make their jobs more manageable, top managers chose to eliminate as much diversity and interdependence
as possible. They surrounded themselves with other managers
who were just like themselves. They organized themselves
in rigid semiautonomous departments or divisions, and in-
sisted that communication only go up and down the hierarchy

(thus minimizing lateral interdependencies). Such actions usually did eliminate many conflicts and made life at work easier for them in the short term. But such actions always undermined performance in the long term. In some cases, the increasingly mediocre products and services produced by such firms drove customers to their competition. In other cases, new international competition attracted customers with more creative products at a better price. But in both situations the results were similar; increased competition reduced income and revenues, thus increasing internal interdependence among departments that were forced to fight for limited resources. Weak leadership was unable to manage these conflicts in a productive way. That, in turn, led to more bureaucratic infighting, parochial politics, and destructive power struggles. The energy wasted in these pathological power processes then reduced efficiency still more, raised costs, killed what little innovation existed, and alienated much of the work force. All this produced even more conflict and an even more difficult situation to manage.

These two paths, the one taken by today's ailing bureaucracies and the one taken by today's excellent corporations, highlight the challenge we now face (see Figure 3–1). It seems clear that trends beyond our control are creating a more socially complex world of work, which, in turn, is producing more conflict and potential conflict. If this is handled well, the benefits are impressive. Original thinking, creative solutions to problems, and innovative products and services make organizations more effective. They also make life in organizations more exciting and interesting. Conversely, if we do not handle social complexity well, the costs are significant. Bureaucratic infighting, parochial politics, and destructive power struggles reduce efficiency, raise costs, kill innovation, alienate people, and frustrate nearly everyone.

One of the greatest challenges of our age, at least in my opinion, is helping work organizations to get into and stay into the right-hand path shown in Figure 3–1. And that demands competent leadership.

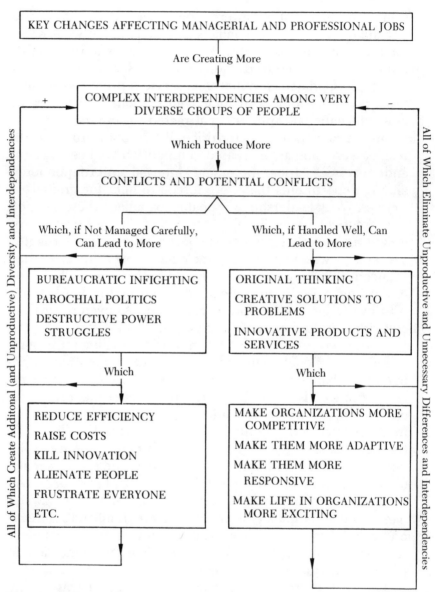

FIGURE 3–1

II

The analysis presented thus far suggests that if we expect the organizations that dominate our world today, and that will dominate tomorrow also, to behave in effective and responsible ways, it is essential that (1) we don't allow them to become so complex that they are unmanageable, and that (2) we staff them with people who are willing and able to cope with the complex social milieu that is a reality in these organizations. Such staffing goes far beyond just the top few jobs; it involves all jobs that have power gaps and thus demand leadership. Having a Winston Churchill or a Thomas Watson in the number one job certainly helps. But by itself, that is insufficient. Most people in professional, managerial, and technical jobs must also be skilled at managing the complex set of interdependent relationships that come with their jobs. And they must see this activity as a central part of their jobs. Competent technical work from these people, in engineering, accounting, marketing, or whatever, although absolutely necessary, is no longer sufficient.

Far too many people today ignore this network management activity. They prefer, and have been taught, to focus on the technical aspects of their work. When others don't automatically cooperate with them, they tend to see the problem as entirely the other party's fault. When others ask them for help, they quickly resent not being left alone to do "their jobs." And when their performances are rated lower than their own evaluations, which is almost inevitable, they usually conclude that they are the victims of "politics."

In staff roles, this means we do not need a lot of autocratic "experts," but rather people who think of their jobs as providing leadership in some technical area, even though the people they have to lead do not report to them. In lower- and middle-management ranks, this means we do not need the cynical jungle fighters, the autonomy seeking craftsmen, or the super-conforming and uncreative organization men that Michael Maccoby, correctly I believe, says are so prevalent today.[3] Instead we need people who see their roles as those of actively leading subordinates, peers, bosses, and outsiders to achieve responsible results within their domains of activity. And at the very top levels in organizations, this means we do not need financial analysts who want to serve only the interests of stockholders or bureaucrats who serve only the interests of other entrenched bureaucrats or salesmen who "give away the store" for the sake of customer relations and sales volume. Instead we need people who are willing and able to serve the interests of *all* the stakeholders involved.[4]

The traditional entrepreneur is also not the answer, as some seem to think. Such people tend to be very good at managing relationships with customers, suppliers, and financial backers. Really successful entrepreneurs are also good at managing subordinates. But traditional entrepreneurs are rarely any good at managing relationships with people inside their firms who are outside their chain of command. And they aren't very good at getting along with bosses. They are temperamentally conditioned to see staff in other departments and bosses as bureaucratic enemies. This is a key reason why they are willing to take the major career and financial risks associated with trying to start their own firms.

What *is* needed—because of increased interdependence— is a much larger number of people who have leadership skills, broadly defined. A century ago, only a few thousand people held jobs that demanded that they manage a large number of interdependent relationships. Today millions do. And because of the greater diversity, the kinds of leadership skills needed are much more complex. Leading one hundred people who all have the same basic goals, values, and perspectives is one thing. Heading a similar-sized group that is composed of twenty warring factions is something else completely.

The relevant skills are both cognitive and interpersonal in nature. They involve the capacity to assess correctly differences among people in goals, values, perceptions, and stakes; the ability to see the subtle interdependencies among those people; and the capacity to identify the implications of this diagnosis. These skills also involve an ability to implement these judgments by successfully influencing what is often a large and diverse group of people. These are the skills of leadership in an organizational society.

Part II of this book will explore these leadership skills in some depth. It will nevertheless help, I believe, if we briefly summarize them now. This summary will not attempt to justify or amplify the conclusions. That will have to come later.

III

Managing complex diversity and interdependence in an effective and responsible way requires, first, sufficient power to make up for the power gap inherent in leadership jobs and then, second, the willingness to use that power to manage all the interdependencies in as responsible a way as possible.

The power one needs comes, of necessity, in many forms. It has multiple bases, including ones associated with information or knowledge, good working relationships, personal skills, intelligent agendas for action, resource networks, and good track records.

The truism "knowledge is power" certainly applies to many jobs today. But the type of knowledge that is particularly important in leadership jobs is not the kind one finds in books or in educational programs. It is detailed information about the social reality in which the job is imbedded.

There is no way that one can perform well in a leadership job today without a keen understanding of the diverse and interdependent milieu surrounding the job. This means knowing who *all* the relevant parties are, even though there may be thousands of them. It means knowing the different perspectives of all the relevant groups: what they want, how they look at the world, and what their real interests are. It means knowing where the various perspectives are in conflict— where important differences lie. It means knowing what sources of power each group has to pursue its own interests, and to what extent they are prepared to use that power.

This information, along with a sensitivity to its importance, is key to sensible decision making. It allows one realistically to answer questions like: whose cooperation will be needed to implement any idea under consideration? Whose compliance will be necessary? Will any of these people be inclined to resist cooperating or complying? If yes, why? How strongly are they likely to resist? Am I in a position to reduce or overcome this resistance? Which ideas, then, are feasible? Are any of those feasible in everybody's best interests? If not, why not? Who has to pay what cost? Without answers to these questions—answers that do not come automatically with most jobs—one walks blindly through a minefield.

But information alone is never enough. You can know precisely what should be done, and yet not be able to do it, unless you have access to those whose cooperation and compliance is required, unless they are willing to listen to your point of view, and unless they are inclined to believe what you say. In other words, one also needs the power associated with credible relationships with most of the parties involved. This means cooperative relationships with bosses, subordinates, subordinates of subordinates, peers in other parts of the organization, outside suppliers or customers—indeed, anyone on whom the job makes one dependent. The greater the dependence, the more important the relationship.

Good working relationships based on some combination of respect, admiration, perceived need, obligation, and friendship are a critical source of power in helping to get things done. Without these relationships, even the best possible idea could be rejected or resisted in an environment where diversity breeds suspicion and interdependence precludes giving orders to most of the relevant players. Furthermore, since these relationships serve as important information channels, without them one may never be able to establish the information base one needs to operate effectively.

Developing all these relationships, especially when there are many people involved, and when those people are physically spread out, can be very difficult unless one has yet another source of power—that associated with a good track record and a good reputation. A credible track record and the reputation it earns can help one develop and maintain good working relationships with others in a fraction of the time that is required if those power sources are absent. In big leadership jobs, where a lot of people are involved, and time is of the essence, the time savings associated with these power sources are enormously important.

Developing and then using all three of these sources of

power, in turn, requires certain skills, skills that serve as still another important source of power. These skills include the cognitive ability to diagnose correctly who really has power that is relevant to any particular issue, to assess differences among people and their roots, and to identify directions of mutual interest. They include the interpersonal skills associated with building good working relationships with many different kinds of people and then maintaining those relationships despite physical separation, limited face-to-face interaction, and the normal stresses and strains of modern life. They also include a wide variety of influence skills—skills associated with knowing precisely how to use information and relationships and formal authority and other power sources in any specific situation. And they include a wide variety of technical skills associated with the particular business or department involved.

These skills, the information base, all the cooperative relationships, and the track record serve to supplement the power sources that automatically come with a job and allow one to do what needs to be done to lead in a highly complex social environment. These power sources allow one to create a visionary agenda for action that charts a course to minimize destructive power struggles, to resolve conflict in creative ways that serve the interests of as many people as possible, as well as to resolve conflicts efficiently. They also allow one to create the resource network that is needed to implement such agendas. They give one the ability to attract good people, needed financing, and new product ideas. They give one the capacity to direct those resources toward one's agenda. In the final analysis, it is this resource network and agenda that are the power sources that enable people to provide leadership.

Using that ability responsibly then requires a willingness to manage the interdependencies associated with one's job in an effective, efficient, and responsible way: not just for short-run gain; not just to advance one's career; not just to serve the interests of only one of the constituencies involved—no matter who that constituent is—not just for customers or employees or even stockholders. One must actively lead those in *all* the relevant relationships, up, down, and laterally. One must be willing to deal with all the challenges these relationships present. And there are many challenges.

Effectively dealing with those outside one's chain of command means being able and willing to overcome a lot of resistance and gain cooperation without formal authority. Effectively dealing with bosses means being able and willing to actually manage a boss. And effectively dealing with subordinates means being able and willing to cope not just with individuals, but with human systems—*systems* comprising the many built-in interrelationships among subordinates.

More specifically, with respect to lateral relationships—that is, those outside the chain of command—effective and responsible leadership demands, first of all, a constant sensitivity to where relevant relationships actually exist. This means always thinking about whose cooperation and whose compliance, among people outside of your chain of command, may be necessary to implement successfully any idea or option or decision that is under consideration. It also requires a continuing assessment of which of those people might actually resist cooperating or complying, why they will resist, how much they will be able to resist, and why they will be able to resist that much. This is essentially an assessment of motivation, perspective, and power. One also needs the skills associated with developing good working relationships despite severe constraints of time and geography. People outside the chain of command are often not easy to see on a regular basis—either because of location or because other priorities limit the time available—and that can make the development and maintenance of relationships a real challenge. And because differences in perspective and in stakes can lead on occasion to fierce resistance from those outside one's chain of command, one sometimes also needs the willingness and ability to use stronger methods needed to deal with that resistance.

This kind of sociopolitical sensitivity and skill has almost always been important in the public sector, especially in elected positions, where there have always been a lot of lateral relationships. But now it is gaining in importance in the private sector, too, as trends continue to increase the number of lateral relationships associated with managerial and professional jobs.

In terms of relationships to bosses, effective leadership demands that one not, in a childlike fashion, abdicate the management of those relationships to the bosses, but that one take active responsibility for the development and maintenance of those relationships. Bosses are too important, yet altogether too human, for one to do otherwise.

Developing and maintaining effective relationships with bosses involves four basic steps. First, one needs to get as much detailed information as is practicable about each boss's goals, strengths, weaknesses, and preferred working style—and about the pressures on him. Second, one also needs to make an honest self-appraisal—about one's needs, objectives, strengths, weaknesses, and personal style. Third, armed with this information, one then needs to create a relationship that fits both parties' key needs and styles, and that is characterized by mutual expectations. And finally, maintaining the relationship then demands that one keep the boss informed, behave dependably and honestly, and use that boss's time and other resources selectively.

I think both the naïves and the cynics among us assume that the only reason people might cultivate and maintain relationships with their bosses is for self-centered political gain. Both fail to see that providing leadership in complex organizations is impossible without support from bosses, and that getting this support does not automatically happen unless one takes responsibility for making it happen. Furthermore, in an age where differences between bosses and subordinates are growing (differences in race, age, nationality, sex, educational background, etc.), and where the interdependent relationships between them are becoming more complex, I suspect that things work out well "automatically" a smaller and smaller percentage of the time.

In terms of relationships to subordinates, effective leadership demands, first, that one realize that one is not responsible for a number of individuals, but instead for a complex human system made up of different people who are tied together in a variety of different kinds of relationships: leading the system then requires not only information on individual people, but also on all the relationships among them.

This type of knowledge helps make up some of the power gap often found in supervisory jobs, but only some. To be able truly to lead subordinates, one needs also to develop as much credibility as possible among as many of them as possible. This means systematically using one's track record, one's interpersonal and intellectual skills, and one's other personal assets to establish a good reputation and to earn their esteem. This reputation must be established not only among one's direct reports, but among as many subordinates as possible, especially those in key positions, regardless of formal rank.

If you are operating from a position of some strength, leadership would then require your use of this power to structure the subordinate system so that the pattern of differences and interdependence fits the real requirements of your overall mission, and not just history, parochial politics, and the like. Strong leadership means creating an environment where built-in conflicts can potentially lead to creative decisions through effective teamwork, and where destructive power struggles, bureaucratic infighting, and parochial politics are absolutely minimized.

And finally, strong leadership in a supervisory position today means keeping the subordinate system in balance and on target through frequent and carefully targeted interventions—interventions that are sometimes direct and sometimes indirect, sometimes hard yet often soft, usually substantive but sometimes symbolic, sometimes participatory in nature, and sometimes fairly autocratic.

In combination, these assets—the power and the ability and willingness to use the power to manage all the relationships in the complex social milieu—can make an enormous difference. They can turn the kinds of stresses seen in the Johns-Manville; Jones, Day; and ABC cases into productive tensions. If more people in those firms had had these assets, especially those people in key positions, the destructive power struggles they experienced could probably have been reduced in scope if not eliminated altogether. People would have recognized the potential conflicts and their underlying roots earlier. Based on that recognition, they would have been able to initiate actions that would have been effective in influencing events to a more constructive conclusion. People's feelings and their career prospects would not have been damaged. Organizational resources would not have been wasted. These assets could have made a big difference.

IV

Developing all the power sources needed to create strong agendas and networks is not easy. It takes time and effort and *constant* attention. With hundreds or thousands of people involved, and with a volume of relevant information that would fill a small library, developing information and relationship-based sources typically takes years of effort. The relevant skills involved are only to a limited degree learned early in life. They are largely refined and developed on the job, through lengthy trial and error, and by watching capable role-models.

Because of all this, the key challenge during the early career years, for those aspiring to leadership jobs, involves establishing the power bases they will need to be able to perform effectively in such jobs. If they are successful, the key challenge will shift at mid-career to using the power they have acquired responsibly, without inadvertently misusing it. And later on, at the end of their careers, the challenge will be to let go of all that power—to turn over the reins of leadership to well-prepared successors. Part III of this book will describe these challenges in some detail. Here is a brief summary of that material:

In terms of the early stages of one's career, the first challenge is to get into an industry, company or job context that fits one's own needs, values, strengths, and weaknesses to some minimum degree. This fit gives important leverage in developing a power base. The fit makes it easier to start developing business knowledge, because that information is perceived to be interesting. It makes it easier to develop good working relationships, because you like and understand the people. It makes it easier to perform well and thus to start developing a track record, because the work seems fun and relatively easy.

The central task during the early career is developing those power sources one will eventually need for leadership. And developing those sources takes time and attention. The aspiring young manager or professional who pays attention to raises and promotions—instead of track record, reputation, business knowledge, good relationships, interpersonal skills, etc.—may get along fine for a while. But sooner or later his myopia will catch up with him. He may even be thrust into an important leadership job much earlier than his peers. But once in that job, he will have great difficulty performing well.

Developing that power base requires particular attention to the speed of job movement. Certainly if one moves too slowly, one will never be able to accumulate the knowledge and relationships, etc. that one will need for an important job. But moving too fast can be even more dangerous. Racing through jobs, the young "star" often does not learn what needs to be learned, develop deeply enough the relationships that need to be developed, or create as unambiguous a track record as is needed to handle a big leadership job someday. And when this happens, a very valuable human resource is squandered.

Twenty or thirty years ago, these issues were of central importance only to those few people who aspired to the few leadership jobs that existed then. Today these issues are relevant to millions of people. Yet I doubt that more than a fraction of those people are really aware of how important these issues are. Perhaps only a small fraction.

For those who overcome these hurdles early in their careers, still another set awaits them in the prime of their lives. A trap into which many successful leaders fell during the 1970s was inadvertently to create a degree of diversity and interdependence—often through acquisitions or internal diversification—that they were not equipped to manage. Big diversification decisions can significantly increase the power gap in key leadership jobs overnight. They can turn jobs that are doable for the current incumbents into impossible jobs. When this happens, one rarely sees the people in those jobs resign.

Instead they manage as best they can. Corporate performance slowly deteriorates. Eventually they retire. Then a new cadre of managers starts selling off or closing businesses until the jobs are once again doable.

Another major trap, one that is related to the first one, is what I have called the "I can do anything" syndrome. After years of success, after getting into a position of considerable power, one is tempted to overlook just how specialized one's power base is—especially the business knowledge and relationship parts of it—and to conclude that one has the skills to lead anyone, anywhere. People who succumb to this disease not only take on hopeless diversification campaigns, they are also sometimes seduced into top jobs in different companies or industries, jobs for which they are completely unprepared. And then—tragically for them and the companies—they fail.

Another challenge at mid-life for the powerful leader is not losing respect for, sympathy for, and understanding of the vast majority of the people in the world who have much less power. When decisions are complex, and when the executive suite rarely brings one into contact with the "unwashed masses," it is easy to lose one's sensitivity to the impact of one's decisions on the "little" people. And when this happens, leadership fails.

Not long ago these traps were relevant only to a relatively small number of people. No longer. Today, and even more so tomorrow, these issues will be challenges for thousands and thousands of people, people, who often are not yet equipped to deal with such challenges responsibly and effectively.

Finally, at the end of a successful leadership career, one faces still more challenges, challenges associated with succession and transition. After years of being in a strong position, some leaders have great difficulty letting go in a graceful and responsible way.

Leadership during the later stages of a career involves, first, picking a good successor and grooming that person for your job. This takes time and effort and careful attention. It also involves the creation of an attractive "retirement" life for yourself. For some, this might mean nothing more than a home near a golf course and spending time with their grand-children. But for many leaders it means an active life in which they can continue to play leadership roles on boards or in religious groups or in community service organizations.

Finally, responsible leadership means a smooth and effec-tive transition—not the kind we read about in cases like Harold Geneen at ITT, or Bill Paley at CBS.

Good succession-planning systems can go a long way in helping with these late career challenges. But most organiza-tions with which I have dealt do not really have good systems in place. Some have a system that works well at the very top. But few have systems that work well lower in the organi-zation. As more and more leadership jobs emerge at lower levels, such systems will become increasingly important.

In a less socially complex world, these leadership, power, and influence issues would be less important and less difficult. But the eras of relative social simplicity are forever gone. The foreseeable future will bring more diversity and interde-pendence. Issues of power and leadership in the workplace will become even more central and important. And I'm not at all sure we are adequately prepared to deal with this.

V

Not everyone will immediately agree with the conclusions just stated. In discussing these issues with people over the past few years, I have encountered three basic types of objec-tions. Let me briefly note these arguments and tell you why I think they are incorrect.

First of all, some people think that the problems of diversity and interdependence should be solved by drastically *reducing* social complexity. Simplify organizational structures, some say, to give people more autonomy and authority. Organize in small units, others argue. Go back and use simpler technolo-gies. Stop trying to serve one hundred countries. In short, radically reduce the diversity and interdependence.

There are two problems with this line of reasoning. First, it does not acknowledge the potential benefits of social com-plexity. Reducing conflict also means reducing the potential for creativity, innovation, and adaptation. Second, this argument ignores the practical problem of reversing all the trends identified in the last chapter. These trends, which are creating more social complexity, are rooted in powerful forces that are often beyond our control.

Of course, some unnecessary interdependence or unhelpful diversity does exist and this can and should be eliminated. Some of the complexity inside organizations is the product of history or specific personalities and serves no current need. I know of a number of firms who could make themselves a lot more manageable by divesting themselves of a few unrelated product lines, by eliminating a few antiquated rules or procedures, and by creating a few more semiautonomous divisions. But these marginal changes, which are practical, will not radically reduce the complexity of the social milieu. Key players in these firms will still need the capabilities listed earlier in the chapter.

A second set of objections to the conclusions drawn here accepts the inevitability and the benefits of social complexity. But this line of reasoning argues that power and leadership skills are not the answer. What is needed, these people say, is just the application of the problem-solving skills that have traditionally been taught in management education. With this application, "rational" decision making would become the norm. People making this argument often blame those running organizations for allowing all the "politics."

There are at least two problems with this line of analysis. First, top management in all but the smallest of organizations does not have the power to impose norms of rationality on all decision making. Too many people and too many decisions are involved, and the issues are too complex. And even if such norms could be imposed, the rational decision-making approach taught in management education would not work in all situations. Methods that stress open discussion of the issues, logical analyses of the options, and so on, take time, often lots of time. Busy people who are forced by interdependence to deal with dozens of such issues daily will not always have sufficient time to use those methods. These methods also demand that *everyone* involved cooperate, a condition that is relatively easy to achieve in a classroom or in the laboratory (where these methods were developed), but is much more difficult to create when highly diverse goals, stakes, histories, and perceptions are involved.

This second objection, like the first, is basically naïve. The third, in contrast, is put forth by the more cynical folks among us. They agree that social complexity is a reality we cannot eliminate, but they argue that managing it is really impossible. Chaos and power struggles and parochial politics will become the norm, and we might as well just accept this fact. The kind of "sophistication" I suggest is important is not needed. Go out and arm yourselves, make your office a bunker, and fight for survival.

Anyone who has been in some of the finest organizations around knows that this objection is off base. These firms are living proof that social complexity, if managed well, does not degenerate into a jungle. Just the opposite, it produces techno-logical breakthroughs, innovative products and services, a healthy return on capital invested, and a good place to work.

There are still other objections. But these are the main ones. You can judge for yourself, as you read the chapters that follow, whether or not they have any merit.

VI

Achieving what I have briefly outlined will not, by any stretch of the imagination, be easy. There are real costs in-volved. But the benefits are so great, it would be insane not to pay the price.

At a personal level, making social complexity work for us means exchanging feelings of frustration, impotence, and alienation for a sense of efficacy and competence. It means making that gigantic percentage of our waking hours that we spend at work more interesting, exciting, and fun. It means more job satisfaction, and for some, more career success.

At an organizational level, this means exchanging bureau-cratic infighting, destructive political activity, and meaning-less power struggles for productive and creative action. In a sense, it means creating the conditions under which firms that want to be excellent can actually become excellent.

And at a societal level, in a world so dependent on complex organizations, it means nothing less than a better quality of life.

THE RELATIONAL
CONTEXT OF WORK

CHAPTER 4

RELATIONS OUTSIDE THE CHAIN OF COMMAND
Overcoming Resistance and Gaining Cooperation Without Formal Authority

M ost of the power gap one finds in professional and technical jobs is associated with relationships outside the formal
chain of command. This is also true in many managerial jobs.
Such jobs make the jobholders' performance dependent on
people other than just their own bosses and subordinates, without giving them much, or any, formal control over those others. This situation is then often further complicated by many
other factors, including: the large number of relevant lateral
relationships that may be associated with such jobs; the geographic dispersion of some of the parties involved; the existence of very large differences in goals and beliefs between
parties; even ambiguity with regard to exactly where all the
relevant lateral relationships exist. These and other factors
make managing those relationships a complicated leadership
task—and a very important leadership task.[1]

I
It is impossible to estimate how many good ideas are abandoned each and every day, the result of difficult-to-manage

lateral relationships. The number is certainly a large one, as is the amount of frustration associated with such episodes.

A typical example of this problem is seen in the case of a young man who was a programmer for one of the firms located in northern California's Silicon Valley. His name was Jerry Cutler, and he was about thirty-five years old at the time of this episode. Jerry had been with his employer for four years, and although he had never completed college, he was a well-respected and well-paid technical specialist in his firm.

Jerry's interest in the medical applications of the type of equipment his company produced first developed in 1978 when his mother-in-law was hospitalized for nearly six months. During that half-year period, he and his wife visited the hospital two or three times each week. What started as short and casual conversations between Jerry and assorted nurses and doctors eventually turned into serious and exciting explorations about important medical needs and emerging technology that could possibly meet those needs at a fraction of the cost of current methods.

Because of these conversations, in the fall of 1978, Jerry told both his boss and his boss's boss he would like to meet with them about an important matter. At that meeting, he reported recent events at the hospital and then showed them rough specifications he had developed for a new piece of medical equipment. The device was essentially a clever modification of one of the company's existing products, a product which was not then used for medical applications.

Jerry's bosses were impressed. They liked both the concept and Jerry's obvious enthusiasm. As a result, about a week later, they gave Jerry permission to allocate up to one half of his time for the following two months to work with the appropriate people in engineering, marketing, and manufacturing in order to develop a prototype of the product and a financial forecast of its economic viability.

Jerry began working on his project with more excitement than he had felt in years. And at first, all went exceptionally well. He was able to get a number of other people in the firm interested in the potential product. Furthermore, the initial market research suggested that a very lucrative market might exist, one in which there was no comparable product.

But after a good start, Jerry began to run into problems. At first the problems were small, but nevertheless annoying and time consuming. For example, the payroll department in accounting returned his expense report, which asked that a neighborhood high school student be paid fifty dollars for spending a total of twelve hours helping Jerry do some metalworking in Jerry's basement shop. Payroll said, "Company policy requires that such requests be approved *in advance* by someone at least at level 7 in the firm." Jerry spent nearly half a day arguing with people in accounting, but to no avail. Eventually he had to get his boss, who was more than a little annoyed, to intervene in his behalf.

The problems began to get more serious starting a month after the project began. One of the managers within the main engineering department called Jerry on a Tuesday afternoon and told him that the engineer who was working on his project was spending "far too much time" on it. He was told that they had "other priorities and deadlines, and I'm sorry, but I just cannot spare him anymore." Another more junior engineer was assigned to help Jerry, but only for a maximum of five hours a week. Jerry complained that the loss of continuity, experience, and hours would really hurt the project. The engineering manager said he was sorry, but that he could do nothing about it.

Jerry complained immediately to his boss, who retorted in a somewhat angry way that Jerry also was spending too much time on the project. Jerry's other responsibilities were being neglected, he said. Jerry left that meeting predictably upset.

The situation got even worse the next day. A telephone call at about 10:30 A.M. informed Jerry that the person in manufacturing who was supposed to be estimating production costs for the new machine was in New York, dealing with a small crisis in a plant. The caller was not sure when this person would return, or how much progress he had made on Jerry's project. Jerry thought about going to his boss for help, but realized that was probably not a good idea.

The next and most damaging incident came three days later. At four o'clock that afternoon Jerry's boss informed him that someone in marketing had redone the market potential analysis based on new data from the sales department. The new forecast projected a market about one fifth the size of the original forecast. Based on this new information, Jerry's boss told him they would have to stop investing time in the project. Other priorities were more important. "Sorry."

Jerry was furious. After investing so much time and energy in the project, he was intellectually convinced of its importance and was emotionally committed to it. Could the company be this stupid, he wondered? Do I really want to work for a company that is this stupid?

At 4:45 P.M. Jerry resigned and went home. His boss called him two or three times the next day, but Jerry refused to take the calls. It took him a week to get over his rage. It took another six weeks to get a new job.

Shortly after he started his new job, Jerry received a call from an old friend who still worked for his previous employer in a programming job. His friend related to him a story that was circulating among some of the people there. The story went like this: An executive in the sales department learned of Jerry's project about three weeks before the project was terminated. According to the story, he instantly disliked the idea, basically because selling the machine would require a knowledge of hospitals and medical purchasing practices that his sales force did not have. So—again according to the story— he got one of his people to develop some very pessimistic numbers about market potential which he sent to a marketing executive, who was also a good friend, along with a note asking, "Why are we wasting research on this project?"

When they learn of a situation like this one, the naïve are usually outraged at the pettiness, the narrow-mindedness, and the parochial thinking of those surrounding the central character in the drama. They see Jerry and others like him as hero and victim. The cynics see him as a sucker, because they expect that others will always act in self-centered ways. They see the project as a failure from the beginning, and they see Jerry as a fool for initiating it.

The truth is that Jerry and people like him are neither fools nor heroes. They are technically capable and innovative, and socially naïve. And this last quality can get them into trouble.

Jerry's regular job allowed him a good deal of autonomy from people in other departments at his firm. It was basically an individual-contributor's job. The project he initiated, however, immediately created a number of important lateral dependencies. Jerry could not do it by himself. He had to rely on help from people in engineering, marketing, manufacturing, and accounting, people over whom he had no formal control. And he needed compliance from still others who were in a position to stop the project.

In a situation like this, it is essential that one recognize this relational aspect of work, and that one actively try to manage it. Jerry didn't. Instead, he focused his time and attention on building a physical prototype of the new product. He saw that as "his job."

The real job in this and similar situations—the leadership job—demands attention elsewhere. It requires:

1. Identifying where all the relevant lateral relationships exist, including those that are subtle and almost invisible (in other words, figuring out who needs to be led)
2. Assessing who among these people may resist cooperation, why, and how strongly (figuring out where the leadership challenges will be)
3. Developing, wherever possible, a good relationship with these people to facilitate the communication, education, or negotiation process required to reduce or overcome most kinds of resistance (developing the tools needed to lead)
4. And when Step Three doesn't work by itself, carefully selecting and implementing more subtle or more forceful methods to deal with the resistance (having the courage to lead)

The rest of this chapter will be spent discussing these four steps.

II

Effective leadership in a job that includes a complicated set of lateral relationships requires, first, a keen sense of where those relationships are. To the naïve ear, this sounds easy, but often it is not. For a number of reasons, lateral relationships are often not very visible. Unlike superior and subordinate relationships, few lateral dependencies are unambiguously identified on organization charts or in job descriptions. Furthermore, they are more fluid and change more often than relationships within the chain of command. Indeed, because the dependence associated with any job is a function of the goals, values, and plans of the incumbent in that job, as those factors change, so does the configuration of the dependence. This means that every new assignment can bring with it a new set of lateral dependencies. Even within an assignment, every significant change of direction can bring with it new dependencies.

A related reason why relevant lateral relationships can be difficult to see is because they are a consequence of activities that, by themselves, are complex and difficult to assess. Managers, professionals, and technical specialists deal with tasks that are multifaceted and nonroutine. As a result, it is often difficult at the beginning of a project to know where you will end up and, thus, where all the relevant lateral dependencies are.

Coping with this reality requires, first of all, constant sensitivity to the issue of whose cooperation or compliance may be necessary in the future. This, in turn, demands a keen sense of where you are going, of what tasks may have to be accomplished, of who will actively need to do something if these tasks are to be accomplished effectively and responsibly, and of who may be in a position to block these needed actions. And because one can never predict the future entirely, coping with the problems created by lateral relationships requires that one be careful not to alienate inadvertently any potentially relevant individuals.

Too few people have this kind of sensitivity today. Jerry didn't. Young people in particular are often oblivious to these issues. And that often gets them into trouble.

Take, for example, the case of a young consultant working for a well-known U.S. consulting firm. He was less than one year out of graduate school, had an impeccable set of credentials, and was by any standard very bright, ambitious, and hard working. He had just started work on a new assignment for a relatively small manufacturing company that wanted help deciding in which product lines it should invest its limited capital. Because it was a small project for the consulting firm (total billing expected to be less than $15,000), a senior consultant assigned only this young man and made it clear that it was important to get the job done quickly and on budget.

The young consultant accepted the assignment with great enthusiasm, because it was the first time he had been given a project of his own. He viewed the assignment as an excellent opportunity to demonstrate his growing competence at business consulting, to make a profit for his firm, and to help a client company.

During the first day the consultant spent working at the company site, the firm's president set up a meeting with most of his managers to provide the young man with information. The president talked about his own impression of what the key resource allocation issues were and encouraged others to share their views. The consultant, who was very aware that he was just about the youngest person in the room, went out of his way to demonstrate his grasp of the issues and his expertise in this area. From the consultant's point of view, the meeting went very smoothly. There was only one somewhat awkward incident, but even that helped demonstrate his expertise.

It seems that about two-thirds of the way through the meeting, a small man in a rumpled brown suit sitting in the back of the room spoke up for the first time. He asked a long and confused question that showed he clearly did not understand what the consultant was talking about. Not wanting to waste time trying to tutor this person in a group meeting, the consultant tried to deflect the question. But the man persisted by asking still another. So the consultant used his verbal skills and wit to put him in his place. It worked. Almost everyone (except the man) laughed, and the small man in the rumpled brown suit shut up.

After the meeting, the consultant met individually with a number of the firm's top managers and quickly determined that the key to his analysis lay in identifying the true costs associated with each product line. He then went to the vice-president of accounting and learned that most of the historical data he needed to determine true costs were not on the computer, but were stored in a number of different idiosyncratic ways in files scattered throughout the accounting department and the plant. By four o'clock that afternoon it became clear to the increasingly anxious consultant that neither the accounting vice-president nor his key aides knew how these files were organized, or even where they all were.

As the prospect of going significantly over budget on this project became a reality, the young man grew more and more nervous. But finally, to his great relief, the vice-president of accounting remembered that one of his other subordinates would be "the one person in the company who will surely know how to find and access those files." The consultant was directed to a small room in the back of the accounting department, to which he immediately went. In that room he found one person. It was the small man in the rumpled brown suit.

To some degree, the young man in this case obviously ran into a bit of bad luck. But the incident, and the consequences, could have been easily avoided. He knew in advance that the consulting assignment would include a data-gathering stage. He also knew that some of the most important information he would need was in the hands of the management of the client firm. In advance, he couldn't know exactly who among the managers would be more or less important in this respect. But he should have realized that until this was clear, he could not afford to alienate any of them. And he clearly could have avoided offending that one manager, while still getting on with the immediate task; he only needed to say something like: "This is an interesting question which I believe will take some time to answer fully. I would be happy to do so now, or to meet separately with the gentleman who asked the question sometime after this meeting, whichever you folks would prefer."

The young man behaved as he did for much the same reason as did Jerry. He saw his "job" as that of an expert who gathers data, analyzes data, and reaches relevant conclusions. He did not think of his job in relational terms, or as a leadership challenge. And he paid a price for that. (The small man simply couldn't remember certain key facts, no matter how hard he tried!)

Problems like this are largely avoidable, but they require that one condition oneself to think routinely and regularly about questions like these:

- What am I trying to achieve in my work? What is my vision of the future?
- What are the key tasks I need to accomplish this year? This month? This week? Today?
- For each of these tasks, whose cooperation will definitely be necessary? Whose cooperation may be necessary?
- Whose compliance will definitely be necessary? That is, who can block or retard the accomplishment of these tasks? Whose compliance may be necessary?

Effective leaders in business and government automatically think along these lines. Our best elected officials, in particular, are highly sensitive to these issues because they have to deal with so many lateral relationships. But most of the rest of us have significant room for improvement.

III

Once the existence of relevant lateral relationships has been correctly established, the next step in responsibly leading people in those relationships involves diagnosing who may resist cooperation, why, and how strongly.

There are literally dozens of possible reasons why even very reasonable people may not be inclined to cooperate in the way we want, even when we think we have mutual interests.[2] People don't cooperate because they have different

priorities and do not have the time or resources to do everything, including help us. They don't cooperate because of limitations in their own abilities, which make it difficult to comply
with our requests. They resist because they have different
assessments of how they might best help. They don't cooperate
because they are simply unaware of what we really need.
They resist because they do not trust us. They don't help
very enthusiastically (like the man in the rumpled brown suit)
because they are angry at us. And perhaps most important
of all, they don't cooperate because they believe they have
different stakes in actions than we do and fear they will lose
something they value in the process of cooperating with us.

The central theme that runs through this list of reasons
why people resist is diversity. Significant differences in stakes,
abilities, priorities, and assessments of the situation can easily
lead to conflict instead of cooperation. And differences can
be great among parties in lateral relationships—certainly more
so than in superior or subordinate relations. The goals, values,
and beliefs of, for example, a mid-level accounting employee
and the mid-level R&D manager to whom he sends reports
will be more diverse than between either of them and their
immediate bosses. These differences, when they involve outsiders such as national union officials, government officials,
or members of the press, can be very large.

Systematically diagnosing the differences involved is a central part of successfully managing lateral relationships. But
all too often people don't realistically analyze the situations
they are in, but instead make either naïve (differences are
minimal, everyone will cooperate) or cynical (differences are
gigantic, no one will want to cooperate) assumptions. Young
people in particular often assume that significant differences
do not, or should not, exist among people working for the
same employer. Assuming a high degree of mutuality of interests, they are surprised and angered when fellow employees
don't see things as they do and don't do what they think is
obviously best. When they encounter a difference of opinion
with a fellow employee in another department, they often
assume that the other person is incompetent or just plain stubborn. They are oblivious to many of the forces creating the

difference of opinion. They fail to realize how easily interdepartmental conflict can emerge in organizations.

To demonstrate this problem and its roots, we often use in our teaching programs the case of Corning Glass Company's Electronic Products division.[3] This division, one of nine line divisions at Corning, manufactured passive electronic components for several markets. In the summer of 1968, all the departments within this organization were fighting with each other, and nearly everyone blamed everyone else for the problem. Product development personnel were angry at marketing people, who, they felt, did not provide them with adequate specifications for new products, and with salespeople, who, they felt, often didn't provide them with customer comments on new products. Manufacturing personnel believed sales was "giving the store away at the plant's expense" by being concerned only with sales volume. They also had "no confidence in the marketing people," who, they believed, "lacked the ability to forecast marketing trends accurately." Marketing, on the other hand, saw manufacturing personnel as "conservative and unwilling to take risks." They were highly resentful of manufacturing's "lack of cooperation and the continual sniping" that came from them. And they were very critical of product development personnel, who, they felt, were always late and not at all responsive to their needs. Finally, salespeople felt marketing personnel didn't "have the capability to do their jobs." And salespeople sometimes even got into shouting matches over the phone with manufacturing people, who, they felt, were unresponsive to their customers' service needs.

To be effective in cases like this one, it is essential to see how the conflicts are rooted in the complex differences involved, and how these differences are, in turn, created by strong formal and informal forces. One needs to see how differences among the departments at this Corning division were, first of all, a function of the organizational structure that created the departments. When people are asked to work only on sales (or manufacturing or whatever) tasks, they inevitably become more sensitive to the needs and problems associated with these tasks, and less sensitive to those associated with other related tasks. Second, the formal measurement and reward systems directed each department toward different key goals. Salespeople were measured on sales volume, manufacturing managers on gross margin (the plants were profit centers), and marketing people on measures of growth and profitability for their market segments. Third, specialized selection and promotion processes left each department with somewhat different types of people. Finally, because the division had been in existence for a number of years, each department had developed its own somewhat different culture, shaped by the different tasks, formal arrangements, and key personalities involved.

The entire situation in this case was made still more complex by differences between the division's business and the corporation's traditional businesses. Because of these differences, some divisional personnel were convinced that corporate executives did not understand their situation and that certain things the division was required to do, such as use a particular type of measurement system, were inappropriate.

Blind to these differences and the powerful underlying forces, the naïve among us often think that all that is needed to get people to cooperate in a case like this is a good "win one for the Gipper" speech. Cynics often think a few under-the-table deals can resolve the conflicts. As the Corning executives involved in this case can certainly testify, life is much more complex. They spent three years of very active effort before making some progress on this difficult problem.

Almost the opposite situation—underestimating mutuality of interest—is common when surface differences are large. Here, an incorrect assessment of the real roots of visible differences leads to an assessment that the other party is "the enemy," and that little, if any, mutuality of interest exists. A good example of this problem can be seen in the lateral relationships one finds more and more frequently these days between managers or professionals and third parties—chiefly the press and the government—that mediate their firm's relationship with the public. Because the parties involved often seem so different in outlook and goals, each side has a tendency rather cynically to attribute very selfish motives to the other, and an adversarial relationship develops—a relationship that does not serve well either of the parties involved.[4]

Indeed, adversarial relations between managers and the press can seriously hurt the firm for which those managers work and can even harm the managers personally, in terms of reputation or sales volume, when critical and not entirely accurate reports are made to an audience of millions. I have talked to dozens of businesspeople who feel they have been "burned" this way. At the same time, these adversarial relationships hurt the press as well. Reporters need information; it is the tool of their trade. Because they often have poor relations with businesspeople, they sometimes have tremendous difficulty getting information on business stories. Most of the reporters I know complain bitterly about the difficulty of getting businesspeople to talk to them and about how that wastes their time, reduces their output, and jeopardizes their reputations, since they have to publish stories based on very limited information, which can thus be inaccurate.

Conversely, the businesspeople I know who are most effective in dealing with the press, and the most successful business reporters I have ever met, both seem to have a keen sense both of business-press differences and of their mutuality of interests. They then use their sense of the mutuality of interests to guide their actions. They use their knowledge of differences to predict when resistance and conflict may emerge. And when resistance cannot be entirely avoided, they are careful to assess just how strongly the other party can resist. This is an exercise in assessing power.

Assessing power correctly is an important leadership skill because a position (where one fits in the formal hierarchy) is only one of many sources of power in a modern organization. Other important power bases include information and the control of information channels; the control of tangible resources such as money, machines, or people; a track record that demonstrates expertise in some area; personal qualities such as energy, intelligence, or interpersonal skill; and good relationships with important others.[5] Any of these might be relevant in a specific situation and may allow a person to resist strongly one's efforts to obtain cooperation.

Over the years, I have encountered literally hundreds of examples of capable people underestimating, to their detriment and the detriment of their organizations, how much others they depended on in lateral relationships would resist cooperating with them on something or how able they would be to resist. And in the process, I've seen new product development efforts, quality-of-work-life programs, new MIS systems, structural reorganizations, merger and acquisition efforts, and much more, simply fail. At the same time, I have also seen similar efforts successfully implemented, despite a lot of initial resistance from powerful interest groups, simply because the people leading the efforts correctly anticipated where the biggest problems were likely to be. Likely resistance from powerful individuals or groups does not have to kill innovative new products or programs. But it must be correctly anticipated in advance.

IV

Armed with a keen sense of where problems may develop because of lateral relationships, effective leadership then requires that one select and implement strategies for eliminating or overcoming these problems.

Probably the single most common strategy effective managers, professionals, and technical experts use in this regard is relationship development. That is, they work to develop a personal relationship with the relevant other parties and then use that relationship to facilitate the communication, education, or negotiation process required to reduce or overcome most kinds of resistance to cooperation.

Good working relationships can be developed and maintained in any number of different ways. In the most common method used, one uses one's understanding of the other party to meet dependably certain of their expectations and needs. When you have done this for a while, the other party naturally begins to trust you, to listen more carefully to your ideas and advice, and generally to want to reciprocate by meeting your needs.

Given enough time and access, most people could develop

good working relationships with those outside the chain of command with whom they must interact. But the challenge posed by jobs in today's organizations is that one seldom has enough time or access. This was a big part of Jerry's problem. He certainly would have been more successful with his product development project if he had had the time and access to develop good working relationships with all the people in engineering, manufacturing, marketing, and accounting that became involved in his effort. But any number of factors conspired against his being able to do so: There was time pressure involved, the number of relevant others was not small, and those others were not physically located near Jerry's work area.

This problem can often be found in its extreme form in sales jobs. Take, for example, medical salespeople for pharmaceutical firms.[6] Like sales personnel in many businesses, these individuals are usually given geographic areas. They are then held responsible both for helping to create a demand for their products by calling on physicians in their territories, and for making their products available in distribution channels by calling on pharmacies and wholesalers. Although the size of the territory can vary a great deal depending on the size of the firm and other factors, it would not be unusual for an ethical drug salesperson to have about 200 different doctors and wholesalers that he or she was expected to serve. (There could be well over a thousand pharmacies, too.) Generally, these customers tend to be very busy. Doctors are reluctant to give pharmaceutical salesmen more than five to ten minutes because of patient loads. Wholesalers often see one hundred or more salespeople per week and are thus not inclined to give any one much time, either.

Under these circumstances, salespeople find themselves spending the majority of their time either traveling from one customer to another, or waiting to see a busy customer. In between these periods of driving and waiting, they may have five or ten minutes to influence someone's feelings about their products—someone who sees them only for a few minutes each month and who, in many cases, will be naturally suspicious of "salesmen."

Coping with situations like this requires careful thought, planning, and organization. A "Bill Moyers' Journal" documentary, first shown on PBS a few years ago, demonstrates this well.[7] The show focuses on David Rockefeller, who was then chairman of the Chase Manhattan Bank. Moyers and a film crew accompanied Rockefeller on an important business trip to Europe. On the trip, which only lasted two weeks, Rockefeller met and talked to hundreds and hundreds of people—people whose help and cooperation he needed in different ways to fulfill his responsibilities as chief executive officer at Chase.

To help him cope with the fact that there were many people, that they were spread out in many locations, and that there was little time available, Rockefeller and his staff did the following. First, they began planning the trip nearly *a year* before he actually took it. They took great pains to see that the right people were in the right place at the right time in the best setting to facilitate the work that needed to be done. They scheduled Rockefeller's time in great detail and with great care.

They also prepared for Rockefeller a set of books—one for each country he visited—containing the names of all the people he would be meeting that he had met before, along with some information about these people and about when and where Rockefeller last met them. Rockefeller then read the appropriate book on the plane before visiting each country. In this way he was armed with information that helped him to reestablish quickly a relationship with people, some of whom he had not seen in years, and some of whom he had met only once.

Even when he met people he had never met before, his staff seems usually to have provided him with information to make the relationship-development and orientation process less burdensome. And Rockefeller, after many years of experience, clearly knew how to use his charm, wit, and other personal qualities to turn strangers into friends very quickly.

The Rockefeller example may seem a bit extreme. But all the successful salespeople I have known have used similar techniques to cope with the difficulties inherent in their jobs.

The naïve usually find this kind of behavior insincere and manipulative. Cynics smile knowingly, assuming that this is what all human interaction at work is like. Both miss the point. Neither sees how certain circumstances, but not all, require this type of carefully planned and executed interaction for the good of all the parties involved.

For example, these techniques are completely inappropriate in a job which has few lateral relationships associated with it, where the differences between the people involved are small, and where the people are all located in the same physical setting. In such a situation, the application of these techniques truly is insincere, manipulative, and unnecessary. But in jobs with structures similar to the sales jobs we have been discussing, the kinds of actions taken by Rockefeller are a part of what effective leadership is all about. Such actions represent realistic adaptations to the relational context of the job.

V

A good relationship coupled with good communication can overcome most but not all forms of resistance that one can encounter in lateral relationships. In some jobs, the structure of the relational context can create particularly strong or stubborn resistance. And when this occurs, one sometimes needs to use more complicated or more forceful methods, despite the fact that using them introduces an additional element of risk.

Take, for example, the job of product manager in a firm like General Mills or General Foods.[8] Such a job has revenue and income responsibility for some product line. This arrangement makes the jobholder dependent on all the people who make those products, who advertise them, who sell them, who distribute them, and so forth. There are usually thousands of these people. Yet none reports to the product manager. Instead, these people are located in different chains of command or even outside the product manager's firm. For example, the people who manufacture the products are a part of a large manufacturing organization, and those who sell them are a part of a separate sales force. The product manager has no formal authority over any of them.

A typical product manager's lateral relationships are further complicated by two other factors. First of all, the people with whom he deals make or sell or distribute many products, not just his own. As such, they do not always give a particular product the priority that he wants or needs. Furthermore, these other people are usually not located physically close to him. So he is not able to walk down the hall or up the stairs and have a quick talk with them about something.

Working in this kind of a situation, a product manager is confronted with many difficult lateral relationship problems and questions: How can you get hundreds of salespeople, over whom you have no formal authority, and who are spread out all over the country, to take the time to implement properly a new promotional campaign for a product, despite the fact that the product is only one of fifty that they handle? How can you get manufacturing managers to be fair in their allocations of overhead to your product, without taking actions that might inadvertently alienate them? How can you get busy advertising executives, who serve many clients, to make that extra effort so that the next set of TV commercials are just right without being perceived as being unreasonable or a pest?

A good product manager should be able to deal with these problems most of the time by using the relationship development and communication methods previously described. But occasionally the conflicts will be so large and the resistance so stubborn that more is needed.

Take, for example, the case of a product manager who ran into a stone wall of resistance from one of the plant managers with whom he worked. Normal procedures within his firm required that a number of people, including the relevant plant managers, "sign off" on all new product ideas. In this case, the product manager had lined up everyone he needed, except for one plant manager, to proceed with a new product idea about which the product manager was very excited. He was convinced this new product was in everyone's best interests—his own, the company's, the plant managers', and his customers'. But after a number of discussions with this manu-facturing executive, the product manager concluded that there was no way he could persuade this person of the merits of his proposal—at least within the time constraints involved. (He did think that if he had more time, he would have broken through the barriers.) The basic problem was that the plant manager had once worked in a plant that had had great diffi-culty with a similar type of product. As a result, he reacted in almost a knee-jerk way to the proposal.

To overcome this almost emotional resistance to his idea, the product manager devised and implemented the following plan. First, he got someone that the manufacturing manager respected highly to send that manager two market research studies that were very favorable to the new product, along with a note saying (something along the lines of) "Have you seen this? I found them rather surprising. I am not sure if I believe them, but still . . ." Then the product manager got a representative of one of the company's biggest customers to mention casually to the plant manager in a phone conversa-tion that he had heard a rumor about the new product idea and was "glad to see you guys on your toes as usual." Next, he arranged for two industrial engineers to stand near the manufacturing manager prior to a meeting and talk about the favorable test results on the product. Then the product manager set up a meeting to talk about the product, and in-vited only people he was sure the plant manager liked (or respected) and who also felt favorably about the new product. A day after that meeting, he asked the manufacturing man-ager to sign off. And he did!

This kind of approach is clearly manipulative, at least by most people's standards. And it is risky. If the plant manager ever concluded that he was being "manipulated," he might well react very negatively. But there are times—and that's the point—where one needs to take such a risk if one is going to provide leadership on some issues (such as that new product development idea).

On even rarer occasions, one can encounter still more forceful resistance to cooperation, and one must employ even more forceful and even riskier methods. A good example would be Harold McGraw's successful efforts a few years ago to stop American Express from taking over his firm.[9]

Roger Morley, the president of American Express, and chairman James Robinson III, had been aggressively looking for merger and acquisition candidates when they concluded that McGraw-Hill was a good possibility. When it became clear that Harold McGraw, the chief executive officer and grandson of the company's founder, was not interested, they persisted anyway. In the winter of 1978–79, they bid thirty-four dollars a share for McGraw-Hill, and later increased the offer to forty dollars.

Harold McGraw became incensed by the hostile takeover attempt. He was convinced it was not in his firm's best interests. So he did the following: First, he put full-page ads in the *Wall Street Journal* and in *The New York Times* accusing American Express of lacking "integrity and corporate morality" because of the way they went about making the offer. Then he got the banking committee of the United States House of Representatives interested in exploring American Express's exemption from the Bank Holding Company Act, which permits the firm to operate in a variety of businesses. He also began gathering information about an allegation that American Express violated U.S. anti-Arab boycott laws. And he raised several questions about the future editorial independence of McGraw-Hill's many magazines in the event of an American Express takeover.

At first, American Express tried to convince those other members of the McGraw family who held large blocks of stock that their offer was in everyone's best interests. But they failed. According to *Fortune*, John McGraw, who owned about one hundred thousand shares and sat on the firm's board, "was persuaded by the arguments marshalled by the company lawyers: mainly that because of the questions being raised in Washington by the Federal Communications Commission over transfer of McGraw-Hill television licenses and by congressional banking committees, the merger would never have gone through and McGraw-Hill would have been wounded by the long battle." Eventually, American Express backed down, after having spent $2.4 million in the process.

Coercive strategies are clearly risky because they invite retaliation. But as the McGraw-Hill case suggests, they are sometimes necessary as a last resort. Great leaders throughout history have almost always been willing to put up a good fight, if fighting is the only way to achieve an important objective. And sometimes, although not very often, coercion is the only alternative.

VI

The basic approach presented in this chapter for handling lateral relationships, both outside the firm and within, will probably work in the vast majority of situations. But there does come a point when the number of such relationships and the differences among the parties involved become so great that the situation becomes unmanageable. Leadership becomes, for all practical purposes, impossible.

When this happens, the only real solution to the problem involves reducing the number of lateral relationships or the diversity of the parties involved. Inside an organization, this often means breaking large, highly specialized, functionally structured units into smaller, more self-contained, and more autonomous units. Dozens of large U.S. corporations have been trying to do exactly this, usually calling the change "decentralization" or "divisionalization." Outside of organizations, reducing lateral dependencies takes many forms. Getting legislators to reduce the power of government and setting up multiple sources of supply for all important purchased products or services would be two common examples.

There are people who believe, or want to believe, that these kinds of moves can take us back to the world of work of a half century ago. They cannot. At best, they can turn hopelessly difficult situations into ones that can be managed effectively—if competent leadership is present. But *nothing* can make up for a lack of competent leadership. Nothing.

CHAPTER 5

RELATIONS WITH SUBORDINATES
Coping with Dependence on a Complex Human System

There is probably no other subject in this book that has received more attention elsewhere than the topic of this chapter—the relationship of a boss to his or her subordinates.[1] Unlike the issues in the last chapter, the issue of relations to subordinates has been widely written about, usually under the subject heading of "leadership"; and everyone in a supervisory position recognizes that managing relationships to subordinates is a part of his or her job. Nevertheless, because people often do not appreciate the complexity of the social milieu inside modern organizations (just as most of the traditional leadership literature does not [2]), they often naïvely underestimate just how difficult it is to lead subordinates effectively, efficiently, and responsibly.

Among people who have little or no experience in supervisory positions, I think it is common to think of relationships to subordinates as being like lateral relations, except that you have some formal authority to direct the other parties. As such, relations to subordinates somehow seem easier to handle, because you have more control.

The reality is that relations to subordinates can be just as difficult to handle as are those outside the chain of command. But the nature of the difficulties involved tends to be somewhat different. Supervisors are usually considerably more dependent on key subordinates than on anyone outside the chain of command. Those key subordinates can therefore create special problems and require special attention. In addition, one usually finds much larger interdependencies among subordinates than one typically sees among one's peers and outsiders. This means a supervisor is highly dependent on a complex human *system* of subordinates. This systemic quality of relations among subordinates creates additional special challenges, challenges that must be successfully met if one is to provide leadership in any supervisory job. They are challenges that can be very difficult even for experienced and successful managers.

I

The manager of a small division (110 employees) in a large U.S. corporation once described to me the following situation, variations of which I have heard many times. It seems about six months after he started running that division evidence began to appear suggesting that one subordinate, the vice-president of marketing, was not performing well. Objectives that both he and the division manager had agreed upon were not being accomplished in a timely fashion. More frequent conflicts were beginning to emerge between this person and two of the division manager's other subordinates. Advice from the division manager to this person, regarding what the manager thought was needed, often seemed to be ignored. Although it was not entirely clear how much all this was hurting the division's performance, the manager realized he had a difficult problem on his hands because this subordinate was in charge of the one department (marketing) which was particularly central to the division manager's emerging strategy for the division.

In thinking about this situation, the division manager found himself confronted with numerous questions. First of all, could this subordinate ever perform his job to the manager's satisfaction? If not, should the division manager fire him or transfer him into another job in the firm? If he did move him, where should he look for a replacement? And how long would it take to find a replacement and get him or her up to speed on the job? If the division manager decided his current marketing vice-president could eventually do the job, how long would it be before his performance was acceptable? What would be the costs and risks associated with inadequate performance in the interim? And exactly how could he help the person during this period and get his other vice-president subordinates to help also?

The division manager found none of these questions easy to answer, beginning with the very first one. That is, it was not obvious to him whether the subordinate could or could not really do the job. He found this judgment difficult for many reasons. First of all, the division manager's career experience prior to his first general management job was in finance. He had never worked in marketing and didn't have the same "sense" for marketing experts that he had for financial specialists. Also, it was not entirely clear how much improvement was necessary. Marketing performance in the short run was difficult to measure, and in discussions with his marketing subordinate, the division manager found that they tended to see things differently in this regard. The subordinate felt he was doing a good job under difficult circumstances and that his performance would clearly improve over time. The division manager was not convinced this was true but had no objective way of proving his point.

In considering the problems associated with giving the subordinate three to twelve months to improve his performance, the division manager could see many significant risks. At one extreme, if the subordinate failed—which the division manager considered a distinct possibility—his entire strategy for the division could be in jeopardy. But even if the subordinate could do the job, giving him enough time and support would be difficult. The division manager was already getting pressure from some of his other subordinates and their people to "do something" about the "marketing problem." Because these others also had to depend on marketing, they wanted a solution as fast as possible. They were not inclined to sit back, wait patiently, and be cooperative. Trying to force them to do so could strain the division manager's relationships with them, and create still other problems.

Considering the alternative approach, the division manager was able to identify just as many different problems. If he fired or demoted the manager, he risked the establishment of bad or strained relationships with all those people in marketing who felt their boss was doing at least an adequate job; and he knew that some people felt this way. Furthermore, he would then have the problem of finding a replacement, which could be difficult, since he saw no obvious candidate within the division. Bringing in someone from the outside could take three to nine months. And he knew that outsiders brought in at high levels in an organization often do not work out very well.

If he had been less dependent on his marketing subordinates, he would have had a much less difficult problem, since the division's performance (and his own) would not have been as much on the line. Likewise, fewer differences (less diversity) between himself and his marketing vice-president would have made it easier for him to know what to do when problems arose and to convince others in marketing that his decisions were just. In addition, less diversity and interdependence among his subordinates would have stopped the marketing problem from creating problems for so many others and would have helped those others to be more sympathetic and cooperative.

The division manager in this case decided not to fire the marketing vice-president. For five months he tried in every way he could to help this subordinate. But results did not improve, and an increasing number of problems and conflicts began to emerge both inside the marketing department and between marketing employees and others in the division. For example, based on a report prepared by a market research analyst, the product planning group in the division spent

nearly 30 percent of its budget for the year and then discovered that the analysis in the report was faulty. Nearly half
the employees in the division got into the argument that followed this discovery. For a two-week period, almost all the
division manager's time was spent trying to stop the teeth-
gnashing and finger-pointing.

During the sixth month, some of these problems became
visible both to corporate headquarters and to a few of his
larger customers. Faced with having to explain to his own
boss and some customers what was happening, having to deal
with an increasingly unruly set of subordinates who wanted
the marketing vice-president out, having to cope with a growing number of squabbles among lower-level employees, and
having to put up with an increasingly political climate in the
division, the division manager finally fired his marketing executive. The vice-president reacted angrily, and despite the division manager's belief that he had done everything possible
to give this man a fair chance, the division manager still felt
somewhat guilty and awkward. (He reported to me that, in
retrospect, he felt he had waited too long before letting the
person go, but even when he did, it was difficult to do.)

The division manager made himself temporary marketing
vice-president until he could find a replacement, which required four months. During this period, his workweek, which
normally demanded sixty hours, increased to over seventy,
as he had to struggle with some angry marketing personnel
(two of whom eventually resigned), a few disgruntled customers (one of which eventually took his business elsewhere),
strained relationships among dozens of lower-level employees
(a few of whom were creating problems for the division), and
a worried group of bosses (at least one of whom had concluded
that the division manager was not performing his job competently).

Although some might think that this type of situation is
relatively rare, it most certainly is not. Over the past decade,
I've talked to hundreds of people in supervisory roles who
have described similar sets of problems. And what is particularly striking is that, in most of these cases, the people involved
knew what it meant to be an effective supervisor. Like the

division manager in the situation just described, they knew that effectiveness in a supervisory role means having some reasonably clear sense of what you are trying to accomplish, and an organizational structure below you that fits that mission. It means getting the right people into the right jobs in that structure and making sure they have the proper goals and resources to perform their jobs well. It means creating the environment and the culture that motivates people to do well and fosters teamwork when it is needed. It means coordinating important interfaces among subordinates and diffusing unproductive tension among them. And as book after book instructs, it means paying attention to both people and production, not just one or the other. Nevertheless, like the division manager in this example, people who have a general understanding of what effective supervision means still have difficulty making it happen.

To some degree, people can't "make it happen" in supervisory jobs because of the inherent difficulty of such jobs in complex organizations. But just as important, problems occur because managers like the division manager above don't have one or more of the key requirements needed to provide real leadership in a supervisory role. Because of this, they end up operating from a position of weakness, instead of strength; and they find themselves unable to do those things they know are associated with effective supervision. They find themselves unable to provide the leadership they want to provide. This is very frustrating when it happens. It undermines organizational performance. It hurts people's careers.

And it happens all the time.

II

Supervisory jobs are routinely referred to as positions of "authority" because such jobs provide the incumbents with a certain amount of power over subordinates—power in the form of the right to hire or fire, budgetary resources to support subordinates, etc. What is just as routinely ignored is the other side of the coin—the amount of power subordinates as a group have over their bosses.

Subordinate power comes in many forms, the most common of which includes power based on:

- Skills that are difficult to replace quickly or easily
- Specialized information or knowledge that is important and that others do not have
- Good personal relationships, which make it difficult to reprimand or replace a subordinate without incurring the wrath of those other people
- The centrality of the job a subordinate holds to the boss's agenda, and therefore, the large impact of a subordinate's performance on the boss's performance
- Job-related interdependencies between a subordinate's job and other jobs that are important or other people that are important, which make the boss indirectly dependent on the subordinate

Taken together, these factors can put bosses at a relative disadvantage, despite the formal power that comes with the boss's job. They can create a power gap, along with the kinds of problems and dilemmas seen in the case of the division manager.

This kind of situation is far more prevalent than is generally recognized today. Indeed, most people in managerial jobs, at one time or another, experience the frustration of having to live with a moderate-sized power gap. In such a situation, you can know what needs to be done and yet not be able to do it. That, of course, is very frustrating and often leads to pleas of "If only they would shut up and take orders. . . ." The emotion in such pleas is well captured in a cartoon that appeared years ago in *The New Yorker*.[3] The cartoon shows a middle-aged manager asleep in his easy chair, newspaper in his lap, having what his expression suggests is a very pleasant dream. The dream, appearing as a bubble above the executive's head, shows him in the Oval Office surrounded by subordinates who are awaiting his commands. And command he does: "I want you, Hawkins, to establish order and weed out corruption. Feyerdich, you stabilize the currency and the economy. . . . You, Benson, normalize our relations with other countries. . . . Meanwhile, Follmeyer, you take steps to mollify the liberal wing and you, Thorndyke, devise some measure to appease the conservative. . . ." And so on. Ah, if only it were so easy.

Fantasy, of course, does not help one with the power gap in a supervisory job. Just the opposite, it can hurt. What is needed is a realistic appreciation for the dependent nature of the job, and for the implications of that reality.

For example, in the case of the division manager, evidence of his marketing problem existed when he first took the job. Had he been more sensitive to the extent of his dependence on his marketing vice-president, he then could have correctly predicted the potential consequences of that evidence, and during his first month on the job, he could have (1) started looking for a possible replacement or backup for the marketing vice-president, (2) begun developing a strategy for the division that was less dependent in the short term on marketing, (3) approached those other subordinates who were most dependent on marketing and gotten their commitment to help the vice-president of marketing before problems developed and, hence, before bad feelings had begun to develop, (4) worked with key marketing personnel to identify some unambiguous measures of short-term marketing performance, so as to avoid later arguments about how well they were doing, and (5) alerted his bosses to the potential problem and his steps to avoid it, thus eliminating the possibility of an unpleasant surprise for them in the future. In this way, it is possible that he could have prevented many of the severe problems that he eventually did face.

The fact that even experienced supervisors, like the general manager, can still overestimate the power of a supervisory position and underestimate the power gap is significant. This suggests there are important forces in place which reinforce out-of-date and unrealistic notions about managerial work. Forces that we are going to have to find ways to eliminate.

III

Sensitivity to the reality of a supervisory job, although essential, is not sufficient for competent supervision. One also needs the capacity to act on this sensitivity. And that requires power to make up for the power gap.

Effectively leading subordinates demands that one bring many additional sources of power to the supervisory job and that one develop still more clout during the early tenure in the job. That is, one must bring to the job relevant personal skills and abilities, good working relationships, information, other tangible resources, and a strong track record to supplement the power sources that come automatically with the job. And during the first few months in a new assignment, it is necessary to develop even more countervailing power over the many job-related dependencies, often by developing additional relationships and obtaining additional relevant information. Altogether, this can then put one in a strong enough position to be able to do a supervisory job really well.[4]

Part of the reason the division manager had such difficulty is that he did not bring sufficient assets with him to make up for the power gap in his job, nor was he successful in developing the additional resources needed during his initial time in the job. He was a talented individual, but because his career path had been almost entirely within the area of finance, he did not have that much information about the details of other departments, including marketing. He had good working relationships with all those with whom he routinely interacted. But because he had only been in the division for three years, and because he had been in a finance job during that time (a job which did not require him to interact with many people), there were a lot of people with whom he did not have strong, positive working relationships. He did have a good track record and reputation, but it was not exceptional. And finally, because he did not have any mentors or particularly strong relationships in the top management of the firm, he was not in a position to obtain easily a high level of support or substantial resources above and beyond those that came with the job.

The most effective managers I have known have always operated from a stronger position than this. Although it is often not obvious to many of those who know them, these managers typically have strong upward and lateral relationships, and they manage these relationships well. They have a detailed knowledge of their work and their part of their organizations. They command more and better resources—people and budgets—than their less effective peers. They have strong and carefully built track records and reputations which they nurture. They also usually have very strong relationships with their employees, especially those in key jobs, based on either (a) a sense of obligation to the manager, (b) perception of the boss's expertise, (c) identification with the boss as a person and with the goals or values he or she espouses, or (d) simply a perceived dependence on the boss. And they take the time and effort to nurture and maintain those relationships.

A good example of this would be the manager of one of Xerox's divisions, Renn Zaphiropoulos.[5] I first met Renn in 1978 and quickly discovered that by any standard he was doing an excellent job of leading the 600–700 people that then worked for him. He not only displayed a keen sensitivity to the human system for which he was responsible (he is sometimes called the "company psychiatrist"), but his effectiveness at successfully influencing people and events when he sensed a problem was very high. As a result, his division was (and still is as of this writing) growing at 30 percent a year, increasing its technological leadership in its industry, producing innovative and well-received products, and providing an excellent place to work for a growing number of people.

What was particularly interesting about Renn was that he made it all look so easy. He didn't work seventy hours a week like many executives; he normally worked closer to forty hours and was proud of that fact. He didn't spend his days running from one problem-filled meeting to another; he moved with a leisurely pace, often just roaming about the division's buildings talking and joking with people. Instead of obsessively studying numbers and charts and graphs, he planned parties for the company.

The naïve point to Zaphiropoulos as evidence that a laid-back, people-oriented, and humane management style is the key to business success. The cynical usually aren't quite sure what to make of him, so they attribute his success to "luck."

Both tend to be oblivious to the key element which allowed him to be so influential without working seventy hours a week at a frantic pace—and that was his power in that system.

Renn was one of five individuals that started Versatec. Because the firm had been very successful, and because people believed that not a small amount of that success was due to Renn, he had a formidable track record and reputation. That alone gave him considerable power in the firm; many subordinates automatically gave him the benefit of the doubt and cooperated because of that track record.

Renn's power also came from personal relationships with his people. He made a habit of meeting everyone hired by Versatec; he personally conducted new-employee orientation sessions. And he found ways of keeping in touch with people on a regular basis, both by touring the facilities and through special events (such as company parties). In these interactions, he encouraged identification with him and his vision for the company, and he established the kind of strong personal relationships that are common among charismatic leaders.

Because Renn had been with his firm since its inception and because he had worked in related industries all his life, he had an invaluable information base which was also a source of power. He knew the technologies, products, and markets. But just as important, he knew his people, their jobs, where important interdependencies existed, and where differences that could lead to conflict were located. In addition, his many personal relationships gave him control of a broad set of channels for new relevant information.

Because the firm was profitable, Renn controlled not only the basic resources that came with his job, but the discretionary resources that were a product of the firm's profitability. These resources provided yet another source of power that could help him influence events and get things done.

Finally, Renn had any number of skills and abilities that were very valuable both in his industry and in his job. These skills helped him develop and maintain and use the other power sources in highly effective ways. They helped him use his information base to develop a strategically sound agenda for his company. They helped him to mold his relationships

and resources into the kind of organization that could implement that agenda—an organization characterized by (1) the
correct diversity of talent, (2) a structure of interdependent
relationships that made sense in light of that agenda, and,
(3) a common culture which was supportive of that agenda.

The specifics of Renn's situation are, of course, idiosyncratic
to him. But the general pattern is not. Effectively leading a
complex system of subordinates requires power. And all the
highly effective managers I have known have a strong set of
power assets—a reality which I believe leaves many people,
especially Americans, with very mixed feelings. On the one
hand, we like the results a strong leader can produce. It is
managers like Renn that create organizations with few of the
pathological power problems we all hate. They are powerful
enough to create and enforce a culture among subordinates
that does not tolerate parochial politics, that rewards teamwork, that eschews petty bureaucratic behavior, and that
places a premium on personal integrity. Yet at the same time,
we are uncomfortable with strong leaders because of our deep-
seated fear of totalitarianism.

The challenge for many of us, I think, is to learn how to
distinguish more clearly between someone who, although very
powerful, just barely makes up the power gap inherent in
his or her job, versus someone who is so powerful that
he can dominate any job-related dependence. I fear that
many of us today are not very skilled at making this distinction.

IV

Effective leaders, like Zaphiropoulos, use their power on
a continuous basis to keep their subordinate system on track
and moving in the right direction. Stylistically, they do so in
dozens of different ways, including ones that are hard and
soft, substantive and symbolic, direct and indirect, participative and autocratic. They have skills associated with knowing
how to match a particular style to the specific needs of the
situation.

The appropriate use of power in a supervisory position

generally means employing it in a soft and human way the vast majority of the time, a way that pulls people along by asking and informing and persuading. Positive reinforcement works better than negative. Most educated people respond better to requests than commands. And over the long run, pushing approaches can hurt people's self-esteem, reduce their professional effectiveness, and damage them personally.

But at the same time, when push comes to shove, effective supervision demands that one be willing to use one's power in a hard way. The most effective supervisors I have met, unlike their less affective counterparts, don't find themselves being indecisive because of strong guilt feelings, even when they have to fire someone.[6] They often develop a reputation like the one attributed to Jim Treyberg, the chief executive officer at Tandem Computers. "He's loving and caring and all those good Marin County words," says one of Tandem's board members, "but when a tough decision comes along, he's hard and he's tough." [7]

An unusual yet illustrative example of a hard approach described to me a few years ago centered around a division of a large manufacturing firm that had been experiencing serious performance problems. A new manager was put in charge of the division and told to "turn it around" as soon as possible. After spending a few weeks studying considerable data on the situation, which corporate headquarters had gathered, he concluded that major changes were needed quickly if the business was to be saved. Since his predecessor had been unable to get the division's management to make any large changes, he made his first trip to the division in the following risky but, he believed, necessary manner:

- He gave the division's management two hours' notice of his visit.
- He arrived with four staff assistants and with three briefcases stuffed with data and analyses on the division and its industry.
- He immediately called a meeting of the top forty managers.
- He outlined, briefly, his assessment of the situation, his

commitment to turn things around, and the basic direction in which he wanted things to move.

- He made it perfectly clear that the way in which the division was being run was completely unacceptable.
- Next, he fired the four top managers in the room and told them to be out of the building in two hours.
- He then said he would personally dedicate himself to sabotaging the career of anyone who tried to block his efforts to save the division.
- He ended the sixty-minute meeting by announcing that his assistants would set up appointments for him with each of the division's managers starting at 7:00 A.M. the next morning.

Throughout the critical six-month period that followed, those who remained at the division generally cooperated energetically with him.

Effective bosses in modern organizations do not use these kinds of influence techniques most of the time because they are sensitive to the problems associated with the harder methods. Coercion, even in its more subtle forms, invites resistance and retaliation. For instance, in the example of the young manager who took such extreme steps to save the division he was assigned to "turn around," his development and coercive use of power could have led to mass resignations and the collapse of the division. He recognized that risk, however, and behaved as he did because he felt there was simply no other way that he could gain the very large amount of quick cooperation needed to save the division. Unlike some well-educated people, he fully recognized that important methods like persuasion can be very time consuming. And persuasion can be completely ineffective if people are not willing to listen.

Managing dependence on subordinates in a direct way means simply asking, demanding, suggesting, or persuading people to do something in face-to-face discussions, on the telephone, or in written correspondence. Most influential supervisors spend a lot of time in these sorts of interpersonal activities each and every day because they are usually quick and relatively uncomplicated.[8]

More indirectly, bosses can provide leadership in a number of ways. Perhaps the most common method of indirect influence involves the use of scheduled meetings. Through the choice of participants, setting, time, and agenda, some people are very skilled at indirectly influencing a group discussion, which in turn influences one or more of the participants in a desired way.[9] To some degree, virtually all supervisors use meetings in this way, because they can help manage their dependence on subordinates in ways that more direct methods cannot. And some people, such as Harold Geneen, the former chief executive officer of ITT, appear to make certain types of meetings a central part of their entire management style.[10]

Even more indirectly, bosses can influence subordinates by altering some of the basic formal or informal structures that affect people on a continuing basis. They can change the formal organizational arrangements, put in new compensation systems, import a new technology, or prepare a revised statement of corporate goals. They can even attempt to alter their work group's culture and informal relationships. In general, effective bosses do so in order to create a set of behavior patterns among their subordinates that fits or matches or is appropriate in light of the work to be done and the environment in which they are operating.[11]

Indirect methods must be used with considerable sensitivity to how various contextual forces affect the behavior of subordinates. And they must be employed despite their slowness and complexity, because they are capable of achieving results that more direct methods simply cannot. Indirect approaches can influence larger numbers of people than an individual could ever deal with face-to-face, and they can change behavior patterns or attitudes that are difficult to change.

In addition to hard, soft, direct, and indirect methods, the effective management of subordinates usually requires the use of both substance and symbols. That is, effective bosses use information and logic to convince people to do something. But they also use architecture, where they spend their time, where they hold meetings, language, stories, and still other things as symbols to attain people's cooperation or compliance.[12] They do so recognizing that subordinates both think and feel, and that to have a major influence on them, one has to appeal to both their thoughts and feelings.

Effective substantive influence methods require that one use information to convince subordinates "rationally" that some action is consistent with their goals while other actions are not, or that some goal is desirable, or that some belief is "accurate." Influential bosses tend to be very skilled in this regard. They know how to gather, manipulate, and present facts and inferences in highly effective ways.

Symbolic influence methods are quite different, as are the skills required to use them well. Symbolic methods appeal less to reason and more to our feelings. People who are very successful in using such methods tend to be very skilled at sensing how people will react to various words, pictures, events, and settings.

Perhaps the most common symbolic method used by effective managers is "role-modeling." That is, they use their own behavior and dress and schedule as a means of communicating symbolically what they expect from their subordinates. A less typical, but interesting example of symbolic methods can be seen in the decision of growth-oriented McGraw-Hill executives, a number of years ago, to move their headquarters from an "old green building on West Forty-Second Street in Hell's Kitchen," to a building on the Avenue of the Americas next to Exxon.[13] Although the new fifty-story structure cost $84 million, the firm's then chief executive officer has been reported as saying he is "convinced it paid off." He tells a story about how, right after they moved in, while he was walking around the building, he encountered a publisher staring out of a window. The man turned around and said, "Shel, I'm already thinking bigger than I did last week."

Finally, in dealing with subordinates, effective supervision requires that one operate sometimes in a very participative way, sometimes in a rather autocratic way, and sometimes at various points in between the two extremes.[14] In deciding how much to involve subordinates in some issue or decision, supervisors can usefully think about their alternatives as existing on a continuum of sorts, where at one extreme the strategy calls for a clear plan of action, little involvement of others, rapid implementation, and the use of some of the harder influence tactics. This type of strategy is designed literally to mow over any resistance and, in an extreme case, would result in a fait accompli. At the other end of the continuum, the strategy would call for a much slower process of change, a less clear plan at the beginning, the involvement of many people in the design of the process, and the use of softer tactics. This type of strategy is designed to reduce resistance to a minimum. In deciding where on this strategic continuum to operate, it is important to consider at least four major factors:

- What amount and type of resistance is anticipated? (The greater the anticipated resistance, the more difficult it will be simply to overwhelm it.)
- What exactly is your position vis-à-vis the targets of the influence, especially in regard to power? (The less powerful you are, the more you will be forced to use slower, higher involvement strategies.)
- What is the location of relevant data for designing the change and the energy needed for implementing it? (Gaining needed information and commitment requires time and involvement.)
- What specifically are the stakes involved? (The greater the short-run risks to the organization's performance and survival if things don't change, the more one needs to move quickly and unilaterally.)

The exact combination of participatory, autocratic, direct, indirect, substantive, symbolic, hard, and soft methods required in a supervisory job will vary from situation to situation. Thus, the best overall leadership style will also vary.[15] Insofar as most people are not capable of being infinitely flexible in this regard—that is, they can successfully employ certain types of styles that are consistent with their personalities, but not all possible styles—there are some very important career implications here. And we will explore those implications, and others related to the material covered so far, in Chapter 7.

Table 5–1

	The Myth	*The Reality*
Basic Conception of the Job	A supervisory job is a position of authority	A supervisory job is a position of dependence
Relevant Focus of Attention	The people reporting directly to the supervisor (i.e., a small number of people and relationships)	All subordinates working on important tasks, regardless of level or rank and all important relationships among subordinates or between subordinates and others (i.e., a large number of people and relationships)
Key Assets Required to Do the Job	Knowledge about planning, organizing, staffing, directing, evaluating	Sufficient power to make up for the power gap inherent in the job
Key Behavior Required to Lead Subordinates	The basic management processes: planning, organizing, staffing, directing, etc.	A wide range of soft and hard, direct and indirect, substantive and symbolic, participatory and authoritarian approaches applied with great care to fit the needs of the situation.
Other Important Behaviors	None necessary	One must also competently manage all lateral and boss relationships

V

The myths about what effective supervision really means are abundant and powerful. They thrive not only among young people with little experience in organizations, but also among many older and talented professionals who have had little direct exposure to supervisory work.

The differences between myth and reality are huge (see Table 5–1). Only when we are really able to embrace the reality of the situation will we be able to make modern organizations perform as we wish they would.

CHAPTER 6

RELATIONS WITH SUPERIORS
The Challenge of "Managing" a Boss

EFFECTIVELY managing relationships with subordinates and with those outside one's chain of command is almost impossible (even if one is aware of the issues discussed in the past two chapters) without the support and assistance of key bosses. Because of their formal power position, bosses can play a critical role in linking subordinates to the rest of the organization, in securing key resources for them, in making sure their priorities are consistent with organizational needs, and in seeing that they are rewarded fairly for their performance. Providing the kind of leadership needed in so many jobs today is enormously difficult when one's bosses don't play these roles well.

Of course, if everyone in supervisory positions performed with great effectiveness all of the time, then relationships to bosses would not be an issue for us. But such a state is far removed from today's reality. Unfortunately, all too often today, relationships to bosses are a source of conflict and problems instead of a source of resources and help. And that means still another set of relationship-management challenges for people who are trying to provide leadership and to make a difference in their organizations—a set of challenges that are not at all well understood.

I

Few would argue that bosses are unimportant. Yet many people naïvely underestimate what a crucial role bosses can play in helping them to perform well, and enabling them to provide the leadership necessary in so many of today's jobs.[1]

The case of John Reed, Citicorp's new chairman, is instructive in this regard.[2] In 1970, Reed was put in charge of the Operating Group, that part of the bank that performed the physical work of processing business transactions—transferring money, handling checks, etc. He had 8,000 people on his payroll, and a budget of over $100 million, despite the fact that he was only thirty-one years old at the time. He also had a big problem facing him; although the volume of transactions handled by his group had recently been increasing at an annual rate of 5 percent, the group's expenditures had been growing at 18 percent per year for almost a decade. Because his department was still using methods and procedures designed decades earlier, when the bank was smaller and times were very different, expenses had gotten completely out of control. The rising costs threatened the bank's ability to meet its obligation to shareholders, customers, and employees. Something had to be done. Reed was given this big leadership challenge, despite his lack of experience in either banking or in banking operations, because those running the bank felt that someone with a new and different perspective was needed to solve this most difficult problem.

Between 1970 and 1972, Reed and a team of managers that he assembled introduced huge innovative changes within the Operating Group. They reorganized, implemented new information and control systems, altered hiring and compensation practices, and generally implemented a whole new system of management. It was a difficult three years, because they ran into dozens of problems, including a lot of resistance to change, both from within the Operating Group and from the bank's other divisions (who had to rely on the Operating Group to process their transactions). Nevertheless, they managed to overcome these barriers and to get their costs well under control. It has been estimated that in 1976 the cost savings from Reed's leadership accounted for 25 percent of Citicorp's after-tax income! These spectacular results literally set a new norm for the banking industry. Even today, as I write this, some banks are studying what Citicorp did over a decade ago in order to apply those ideas to their operating departments.

Many factors contributed to this success story, the most important of which was John Reed himself. But also extremely important was the support Reed received from the bank's president, Bill Spencer, and its chairman, Walter Wriston.

At varying times during the change process, Reed and his team of managers ran into massive resistance from people who were being inconvenienced in the short run by the changes, from people who were skeptical about the direction in which Reed was moving, and from people who did not like the way their jobs were changing. Altogether, these individuals could have slowed Reed down and even stopped him in some areas, as often happens in corporate change efforts. But Reed was able to overcome the resistance, largely because of his bosses' ongoing and very visible support.

Reed has acknowledged publicly that any number of times "when the sharks saw blood in the water and wanted to strike," Spencer and Wriston moved in and saved the day. The ultimate example of this occurred immediately after the biggest crisis caused by all the changes. In September 1971, a reorganization ran into serious problems, and the "money pipeline" that the Operating Group managed "burst" (something that just does not happen in the banking industry!). The crisis that followed, which took a few weeks to correct, created major problems not only for the Operating Group, but for the other parts of the bank. Just when everyone with a complaint was ready to come down hard on the Operating Group management, Spencer and Wriston found a beautiful way to signal unambiguously that they still supported Reed completely and that they expected others to do so also. In October 1971, when some of the problems caused by this very visible crisis were still unsolved, they announced that Reed's two key subordinates, John White and Larry Small, would be promoted in rank to senior vice-president!

The kind of relationship Reed had with his bosses is not the norm in industry or government today. All too often, problems exist in boss-subordinate relationships, which undermine capable people's capacity to provide leadership in their jobs, and which often hurt the organizations and the individuals involved.

The case of Frank Gibbons and Philip Bonnevie is a perfect example of this. Gibbons was an acknowledged manufacturing genius in his industry and was, by any profitability standard, a very effective executive.[3] In 1973, his strengths propelled him into the position of vice-president of manufacturing for the second largest and most profitable company in that industry. Gibbons was not, however, a good manager of people. He knew this, as did many others. Recognizing this weakness, the president made sure that those who reported to Gibbons were good at working with people and could compensate for his limitations. The arrangement worked well.

In 1975, Philip Bonnevie was promoted into a position reporting to Gibbons. In keeping with the previous pattern, the president selected Bonnevie because he had an excellent track record and a reputation for being good with people. In making that selection, however, the president did not notice that, in his rapid rise through the organization, Bonnevie himself had never reported to anyone who was poor at managing subordinates. Bonnevie had always had good-to-excellent superiors and had never been forced to manage a relationship with a difficult boss. In retrospect, Bonnevie admits he had never thought about "managing his boss."

Gibbons began supervising Bonnevie the same way he treated all new people under his direct supervision. He was vague and sometimes inconsistent with his directions. He was slow to praise and quick to criticize. When Bonnevie wanted him, he was nowhere to be found. When Bonnevie did not need him, he always seemed to be getting into things.

Bonnevie responded to Gibbons first with frustration and

anger, then with withdrawal. Since Bonnevie was convinced he knew what was required in his new job, he decided to get on with it and pretty much avoided Gibbons except when he really needed something from him. He realized that Gibbons might not like this approach at first but hoped that eventually he would be won over. After all, he thought to himself, good performance speaks for itself.

Fourteen months after he started working for Gibbons, Bonnevie was fired. During that same quarter, the company reported a net loss for the first time in seven years. Many of those who were close to these events say that they don't entirely understand what happened. This much is known, however: While the company was bringing out a major new product—a process that required its sales, engineering, and manufacturing groups to coordinate their decisions very carefully—a whole series of misunderstandings and bad feelings developed between Gibbons and Bonnevie. For example, Bonnevie claims Gibbons was aware of and had accepted Bonnevie's decision to use a new type of machinery to make the new product; Gibbons swears he did not. Furthermore, Gibbons claims he made it clear to Bonnevie that introduction of the product was too important to the company in the short run to take any major risks.

Because of such misunderstandings, planning went awry: A new manufacturing plant was built that could not produce the new product designed by engineering, in the volume desired by sales, at a cost agreed on by the executive committee. As a result, the company lost somewhere between $2 and $5 million.

The tragic thing about this situation—and thousands of less dramatic but similar episodes that occur every year—is that it probably could have been avoided. The cost to the company and the high personal price paid by Bonnevie—being fired and having his reputation damaged—were not inevitable, even taking into account Gibbons's ineptness at managing subordinates.

Situations like this can be dealt with effectively if the subordinate involved recognizes and acts on some basic organizational realities.[4] First, a relationship with a boss involves mutual dependence between people who have different backgrounds and different pressures on them; thus, if it is not managed well, neither can be effective in his job. Second because the boss-subordinate relationship is not like the one between a parent and a child, the burden for managing the relationship should not and cannot fall entirely on the boss. Bosses are only human; their wisdom and maturity are not always greater than their subordinates'. Third, because of this, managing the relationship with the boss is a necessary and legitimate part of a job in a modern organization, especially in a difficult leadership job. Finally, to do this requires that one take the time and energy to develop a relationship that is consonant with both persons' styles, assets, and expectations and that meets the most critical needs of each.

This aspect of work, essential though it is to survival and advancement, is sometimes ignored by otherwise talented and aggressive people. Indeed, I have known dozens of people like Bonnevie, who actively and effectively manage subordinates, products, markets, and technologies, but who nevertheless naïvely take an almost passively reactive stance vis-à-vis their bosses. Such a stance practically always hurts these people and their companies.

II

To get the support, information, resources, and help needed from a boss to perform a difficult leadership job in an effective and responsible manner, it is essential to develop and maintain a good working relationship with that boss. People who are successful in this regard typically do the following:

1. First, they find ways to learn about the boss's goals, pressures, strengths, weaknesses, and working style.
2. They are sensitive to their own needs, objectives, strengths, weak spots, and personal styles.
3. They use all this information to help create a relationship that fits both their needs and styles and that is characterized by unambiguous mutual expectations.
4. Finally, they work to maintain that good relationship

by keeping the boss informed, by behaving dependably and honestly, and by using their boss's time and other resources selectively.

In a sense, developing a good working relationship with anybody involves these same steps. But nowhere is it more important than with respect to a boss, because no one typically has more power over you than a boss. When successful, the relationship becomes a form of countervailing power that helps insure that you get the information, support, resources, etc., that you need.

The first step in this process—getting sufficient information on the boss's goals, strengths, weaknesses, working style, etc.— seems obvious enough. But people all too often do not do this. And it creates problems for them.

Consider, for example, the situation in which a top-notch marketing manager with a superior performance record was hired into a company as a vice-president "to straighten out the marketing and sales problems." [5] The company, which was having financial difficulties, had been recently acquired by a larger corporation. The president was eager to turn it around and gave the new marketing vice-president free rein— at least initially. Based on his previous experience, the new vice-president correctly diagnosed that the company needed to gain a greater share of the market and that strong product management was required to bring that about. As a result, he made a number of pricing decisions aimed at increasing high-volume business.

When margins declined and the financial situation did not improve, the president increased pressure on the new vice-president. Believing that the situation would eventually correct itself as the company's share of the market increased, the vice-president resisted the pressure. When by the second quarter margins and profits had still failed to improve, the president took direct control over all pricing decisions and put all items on a set level of margin, regardless of volume. The new vice-president began to find himself shut out by the president, and their relationship deteriorated. In fact, the vice-president found the president's behavior bizarre. Unfortunately, the president's new pricing scheme also failed to increase margins, and by the fourth quarter both the president and the vice-president were fired.

What the new vice-president had not known until it was too late was that improving marketing and sales had been only one of the president's goals. His most immediate goal had been to make the company more profitable—quickly. Nor had the new vice-president known that his boss was invested in this short-term priority for personal as well as business reasons. The president had been a strong advocate of the acquisition within the parent company, and his personal credibility was at stake.

The vice-president in this case made at least three basic errors—errors that are not at all uncommon. He took information supplied to him at face value; he made assumptions in areas where he had no information; and—most damaging—he never actively tried to clarify what his boss's objectives were. As a result, he ended up taking actions that were actually at odds with the president's priorities and objectives.

This kind of problem can be avoided. It simply requires that one *actively* seek out information about a boss's goals and problems and pressures. It demands that one be alert for opportunities to question the boss and others around him or her to test one's assumptions. It suggests that one pay attention to clues in the boss's behavior. Although it is imperative that one do this when beginning to work with a new boss, it is also important to do so on an ongoing basis because priorities and concerns change.

Being sensitive to a boss's work style can be especially crucial when the boss is new. My colleague, Professor Jack Gabarro, once encountered an excellent example of this. It seems a very organized and formal executive replaced a man who was informal and intuitive. The new executive worked best when he had written reports. He also preferred formal meetings with set agendas. One of his subordinates realized this need and worked with the new executive to identify the kinds and frequency of information and reports the executive wanted. This subordinate also made a point of sending the executive written background information and brief agendas for their discussions. He found that with this type of preparation, their meetings were very useful. Moreover, he found that with adequate preparation, his new boss was even more effective at brainstorming problems than his more informal and intuitive predecessor had been.

In contrast, another subordinate never fully understood how the new boss's work style differed from that of his predecessor. To the degree that he did sense it, he experienced it as too much control. As a result, he seldom sent the new executive the background information he needed, and the executive never felt fully prepared for meetings with this subordinate. In fact, the executive spent much of his time when they met trying to get information that he felt he should have had before his arrival. The boss experienced these meetings as frustrating and inefficient, and the subordinate often found himself thrown off guard by the questions that the executive asked.

The difference between the two subordinates just described was not so much one of ability or even adaptability. Rather, the difference was that one of the men was more sensitive to his boss's work style than the other and to the implications of his boss's needs. That is, he was more sensitive to issues such as: how the boss liked to get information (through memos, formal meetings, or phone calls); whether the boss thrived on conflict or tried to minimize it; how he liked to approach problems; and what kind of language and concepts the boss preferred to employ in problem-solving situations.

Some people find it a burden or even distasteful to have to worry about these kinds of issues. But effective and responsible performance in most organizations today absolutely requires this kind of sensitivity.

III

The boss is only one half of the relationship. The subordinate is the other half. Developing an effective working relationship with a boss requires that the subordinate also know his or her own needs, strengths and weaknesses, and personal style.

In terms of self-awareness, nothing is more important for a subordinate than to know his or her temperamental reaction to a position of dependence on an authority figure. Although a superior-subordinate relationship is one of mutual dependence, it is also one in which the subordinate is typically more dependent on the boss than the other way around. This dependence inevitably results in the subordinate feeling a certain degree of frustration, sometimes anger, when actions or options are constrained by a boss's decisions. This is a normal part of life and occurs in the best of relationships. The way in which a person handles these frustrations depends largely on his or her predisposition towards dependence on authority figures.

Some people's instinctive reaction under these circumstances is to resent the boss's authority and to rebel against the boss's decisions. Sometimes a person will escalate a conflict far beyond what is appropriate. Seeing the boss almost as an institutional enemy, such people will often, without being conscious of it, fight with the boss just for the sake of fighting. Their reactions to being constrained are usually strong and sometimes impulsive. They see the boss as someone who, by virtue of his or her role, is a hindrance to progress, an obstacle to be circumvented or, at best, tolerated.

Psychologists call this pattern of reactions counterdependent behavior. Although a counterdependent person is difficult for most superiors to manage and usually has a history of strained relationships with superiors, this sort of person is apt to have even more trouble with a boss who tends to be directive or authoritarian. When such a person acts on his or her negative feelings, often in subtle and nonverbal ways, the boss sometimes does become the enemy. Sensing the subordinate's latent hostility, the boss will lose trust in the subordinate or the subordinate's judgment and will behave less openly.

Paradoxically, individuals with this type of predisposition are often good managers of their own people. They will often go out of their way to get support for subordinates and will not hesitate to go to bat for them.

At the other extreme are people who swallow their anger

and behave in a very compliant fashion when the boss makes what they know to be a poor decision. Such individuals will agree with the boss even when a disagreement might be welcome or when the boss would easily alter a decision if given more information. Because they bear no relationship to the specific situation at hand, their responses are as much an overreaction as those of counterdependent people. Instead of seeing the boss as an enemy, these people deny their anger—the other extreme—and tend to see the boss as if he or she were an all-wise parent who should know best, take responsibility for their careers, train them in all they need to know, and protect them from overly ambitious peers.

Both counterdependence and overdependence lead people to hold unrealistic views of what a boss is. Both views ignore that most bosses, like everyone else, are imperfect and fallible. They don't have unlimited time, encyclopedic knowledge, or extrasensory perception; nor are they evil enemies. They have their own pressures and concerns, and these are sometimes at odds with the wishes of the subordinate—often for good reasons.

Altering predispositions toward authority, especially at the extremes, is almost impossible without intensive psychotherapy (psychoanalytic theory and research suggest that such predispositions are deeply rooted in a person's personality and upbringing). However, an awareness of these extremes and the range between them can be very useful in helping one to identify where one's own predispositions fall and then to understand the implications of that assessment. In some cases, especially regarding career choice, the implications can be extremely important (e.g., highly counterdependent people tend to be happier and more successful in careers as independent businessmen or professionals, where they do not have a conventional boss). And in virtually all cases, understanding the implications can improve a person's effectiveness.

Take, for example, the case of an individual and his superior who ran into problems whenever they disagreed. The boss's typical response was to harden his position and overstate it. The individual's reaction was then to raise the ante and intensify the forcefulness of his argument. In doing this, he chan-

neled his anger into sharpening his attacks on the logical falla-
cies in his boss's assumptions. His boss, in turn, would become
even more adamant about holding his original position. Predictably, this escalating cycle eventually resulted in the subordinate avoiding, whenever possible, any topic of potential
conflict with his boss.

In discussing this problem with his peers, this person discovered that his reaction to his boss was typical of the way
he generally reacted to counterarguments, especially from
authority figures. Because his attempts to discuss this problem
with his boss were unsuccessful, he concluded that the only
way to change the situation was to deal with his own instinctive
reactions. So he did the following. Whenever he and his boss
reached an impasse, he would check his own impatience and
suggest that they break up and think about it before getting
together again. This small change in his approach helped considerably, because when they renewed their discussion, they
usually had digested their differences and were more able
to work them through in a creative and productive way.

IV

As this last example suggests, using a clear understanding
of both parties to create a good work relationship with a boss
means developing an approach, goals, and expectations that
fit both of these parties.

Above all else, a good working relationship with a boss
accommodates differences in work style. A good example of
this can be seen in the case of an individual who had a relatively good, but not excellent, relationship with his superior.
About three months after starting to work for this person,
he realized that during meetings his boss would often become
inattentive and sometimes brusque. The subordinate's own
style tended to be discursive and exploratory. He would often
digress from the topic at hand to deal with background factors,
alternative approaches, and so forth. His boss, instead, preferred to discuss problems with a minimum of background
detail and became impatient and distracted whenever his subordinate digressed from the immediate issue.

Recognizing the difference in style, this person became terser and more direct during meetings with his boss. To help himself do this, before meetings with the boss he would develop brief agendas that he used as a guide. Whenever he felt that a digression was needed, he explained why. This small shift in his own style made these meetings more effective and far less frustrating for both of them and, in the process, improved his relationship with his boss.

Subordinates can also sometimes profitably adjust their styles in response to their bosses' preferred method for receiving information. Peter Drucker divides bosses into "listeners" and "readers." [6] He points out that some bosses like to get information in report form so that they can read and study it. Others work better with information and reports presented in person so that they can ask questions. As Drucker notes, the implications are obvious. If your boss is a listener, you brief him or her in person, then follow it up with a memo. If your boss is a reader, you cover important items or proposals in a memo or report, then discuss them.

Other useful adjustments can often be made according to a boss's decision-making style. Some bosses prefer to be involved in decisions and problems as they arise. These are high-involvement managers who like to keep their hands on the pulse of the operation. Usually their needs are best satisfied if subordinates touch base with them on an ad hoc basis. A boss who has a need to be involved will become involved one way or another, so there are advantages to including him or her at your initiative. Other bosses prefer to delegate— they don't want to be involved. They expect subordinates to come to them only with major problems and to inform them of important changes.

Making adjustments which draw on each party's strengths and make up for each party's weaknesses can also be important. For example, because he knew that his boss—the vice-president of engineering—was not very good at monitoring his employees' problems, one manager made a point of doing it himself. The stakes were high: the engineers and technicians were all union members, the company worked on a customer-contract basis, and the company had recently experienced a serious strike. The manager worked closely with his boss, the scheduling department, and the personnel office to ensure that potential problems were avoided. He also developed an informal arrangement through which his boss would review with him any proposed changes in personnel or assignment policies before they were put into effect. The boss valued his subordinate's advice and credited him with improving both the performance of the division and the labor-management climate.

Finally, developing effective relationships with bosses demands that one make adjustments so as to establish mutual expectations around key issues. Many factors can produce differences in expectations, and those differences can create serious conflicts and other problems.

The subordinate who passively assumes that he or she knows what the boss expects is in for trouble. Of course, some superiors will spell out their expectations very explicitly and in great detail. But most do not. And although many corporations have systems that provide a basis for communicating expectations (such as formal planning processes, career planning reviews, and performance appraisal reviews), these systems never work perfectly. Also, between these formal reviews, expectations invariably change.

Ultimately, it is up to the subordinate to find out what the boss's expectations are, both broad expectations (regarding, for example, what kinds of problems the boss wishes to be informed about and when) as well as very specific ones (regarding such things as when a particular project should be completed and what kinds of information the boss needs in the interim). Getting a boss who tends to be vague or inexplicit to express his or her expectations can be difficult, but it is possible. One can periodically draft detailed memos covering key aspects of work, send it to the boss for approval, then follow this up with a face-to-face discussion in which each item in the memo is discussed. Such discussions can bring to the surface many of a boss's relevant expectations. Or one can deal with an inexplicit boss by initiating an ongoing series of informal discussions about "good management" and "our objectives." Or one can sometimes get useful information more indirectly through those who used to work for the boss and through the formal planning systems in which the boss makes commitments to superiors. Which approach works best, of course, depends upon the boss's style.

Developing a workable set of mutual expectations also requires communicating your own expectations to the boss, finding out if they are realistic, and influencing the boss to accept the ones that are important to you. The key here is to be demanding without being seen as uncooperative or troublesome. Being able to influence the boss to value one's expectations can be particularly important if the boss is an overachiever. Such a boss will often set unrealistically high standards that need to be brought into line with reality.

V

Maintaining a good relationship with a boss, once it has been established, requires a variety of additional actions. Foremost among these are keeping bosses informed, behaving dependably and honestly, and using bosses' time and resources very selectively.

How much information a boss needs about what a subordinate is doing will vary significantly depending on the boss's style, the situation, and the confidence the boss has in the subordinate. But it is not uncommon for a boss to need more information than a subordinate would naturally supply, or for a subordinate to think the boss knows more than he or she really does.

Young employees, in particular, often naïvely assume that "good performance speaks for itself," which then leads them to undercommunicate with their superiors. That is, as long as they think they are doing a good job and that there are really no problems, they tend to communicate little with their bosses. But for "good performance to speak for itself," a boss and subordinate must have 100 percent agreement on what tasks constitute the subordinate's job, on the relative importance of those tasks, and on unambiguous ways to measure the performance of the tasks. And then the boss must easily be able to see how well the subordinate's performance measures up. Few situations in reality meet these requirements.

When there are problems, managing the flow of information upward is particularly difficult if the boss does not like to hear about problems. Although many would deny it, bosses often give off signals that they want to hear only good news. They show great displeasure—usually nonverbally—when someone tells them about a problem. Ignoring individual achievement, they may even evaluate more favorably subordinates who do not bring problems to them. Nevertheless—for the good of the organization, boss, and subordinate—a superior needs to hear about failures as well as successes. And it is possible to pass on this information in ways that are not self-destructive. One can sometimes deal with a good-news-only boss by finding indirect ways to send the necessary information, such as a management information system in which there is no messenger to be killed. In other circumstances, one can see to it that potential problems, whether in the form of good surprises or bad news, are communicated immediately, before they have grown into big and difficult issues.

Few things are more disabling to a boss and will sour a relationship faster than a subordinate on whom one cannot depend, whose work cannot be trusted. Almost no one is intentionally undependable, but many people are inadvertently so because of oversight or uncertainty about the boss's priorities. A commitment to an optimistic delivery date may please a superior in the short term but be a source of displeasure if not honored.

Nor are many people intentionally dishonest with their bosses. But it is so easy to shade the truth a bit and play down concerns. Current concerns often become future surprise problems. It's almost impossible for bosses to work effectively if they cannot rely on fairly accurate readings from their subordinates. Because it undermines credibility, dishonesty is perhaps the most troubling trait a subordinate can have. Without a basic level of trust in a subordinate's word, a boss feels he or she has to check all of the subordinate's decisions, and this makes it difficult to delegate.

Subordinates who waste their boss's limited time and energy undermine a good relationship almost as much as those who are undependable. Because every request a subordinate makes of a boss uses some of the boss's limited resources, common sense suggests drawing on these resources with some selectivity. This may sound obvious, but it is surprising how many people use their boss's time to deal with relatively trivial issues. They do so without stopping to think of the consequences.

The point is: maintaining a good relationship takes effort. For many people, just pausing occasionally to think about the issues raised in this chapter can help a great deal. This means reflecting on these kinds of questions:

- Do I really know what my boss expects of me, both in general and in terms of specific activities in the next week? In the next month? Am I satisfied that these expectations are sensible and fair?
- Does my boss really know what I expect in return? Does he or she know what resources, information, support, and help I need? In the longer run does my boss know my career expectations? Does he or she accept them and thus work on my behalf?
- How well do we get along on a daily basis? Are there many unpleasant conflicts or problems? If there are, what exactly creates these problems? What can I realistically do to help the situation?
- What demands have I made of my boss in the past month or two? How important were the issues involved to the organization, to my boss, and to me? Were any of these instances a waste of time for the boss?
- Of the various dimensions of trust in a relationship, which ones are particularly important to my boss? Have I been particularly trustworthy on these dimensions recently?
- How well does my boss know what I've been doing for the past few months? If he or she is uninformed about certain activities, could this create a problem? If so, what can I do to correct the situation?

VI

Developing and maintaining a really good working relationship with a boss is often challenging. But there are a number of conditions that can make the establishment of such a relationship particularly difficult. They are (1) the existence of very large differences in age, educational background, and values between the boss and the subordinate, (2) incompetence on the part of the boss, (3) powerlessness on the part of the boss, (4) serious differences and conflicts between the boss and others above him or her in management, or (5) the existence of multiple bosses who have serious differences and conflicts.

Bosses and subordinates are always different in some ways. But occasionally the differences will be so large that they loom as a significant barrier to building and maintaining a good working relationship. Take, for example, the case of a fifty-year-old boss with a high school education, thirty years of experience, and little chance of further advancement and his new twenty-four-year-old highly ambitious, MBA-educated subordinate. Or consider the case of a middle-aged female American manager who is assigned to work for a young Saudi.

Serious barriers to developing a good working relationship also exist when the boss is not fully qualified for the job. All organizations have at least a few incompetent bosses. Some have quite a few, and most are not very good at coming to grips with this problem. Feelings of guilt often overcome the decision makers involved. Instead of quickly identifying bosses that are over their heads and correcting the situation, many firms tend to do nothing. These kind of bosses create relationship problems for subordinates in two ways. First, adapting to their styles, especially if they are really in over their heads, can be extraordinarily frustrating. Second, developing mutual expectations becomes complicated by the fact that what they think is needed and what may, in fact, be truly needed by the organization may be two different things.

Related to this last problem, one sometimes finds bosses who are essentially impotent. For whatever historical reasons, often those associated with incompetence, they simply wield very little power. Such bosses create relationship problems for subordinates because they often cannot deliver on their promises. And because their peers and bosses can so easily pressure them into shifting their goals, their expectations of their subordinates can change constantly.

Serious conflicts between a boss and others in top management create still another barrier to good relations between that boss and his or her subordinates. Such conflicts can manifest themselves in many ways. Sometimes the people involved are rivals. Sometimes they have strong and yet different opinions about key company policies. Sometimes they are just very different—in age, background, etc.—and have trouble relating to each other. Whatever the case, these problems can make life all the more difficult for the lower-level subordinate. In attempting to establish a really good relationship with his or her immediate boss, the subordinate can sometimes inadvertently alienate other people. If the subordinate then tries to patch up the problem with these other people, he or she can just as easily alienate the immediate boss.

Another form of the same problem occurs when someone has multiple bosses who have highly diverse goals or who strongly dislike one another. This can occur in matrix-type organizations or in jobs (such as chief executive officer jobs) where the incumbent reports to a board.

All five of these situations are best handled by minimizing their existence in the first place. This means before accepting a job offer, a promotion, or any change in bosses, it is useful to consider (1) the extent of the differences between yourself and the person who will be your boss (is it possible that they are hopelessly large?); (2) whether the boss is at least as competent and powerful as his or her peers, and if not, what kinds of problems that could create for you; (3) if there is more than one relevant boss involved, how well they agree on goals and policies, how well they get along, and whether there are any really strong animosities.

Of course, there will be some cases in which these problems cannot be eliminated by prior analysis—such as when a boss is promoted and someone else is brought in, or when a job is just so attractive that you feel it cannot be turned down. Then, the burden falls on you as the subordinate to do the best you can, applying the ideas discussed earlier in this chapter. And if that doesn't work, then the challenge becomes one of developing a sufficient power base independent of the boss or bosses so that you can avoid being arbitrarily pushed around or exploited.

Although it is far from easy, it is possible to perform admirably in a difficult leadership job despite any of the five problem situations described above. But it requires operating from a position of strength, a position that far too few people are in today.

PART III

THE LIFE CYCLE OF LEADERSHIP

CHAPTER 7

EARLY CAREER
Developing an Adequate Power Base

A general awareness of the issues discussed in Parts I and II of this book can assist one in overcoming barriers to effective and responsible action in modern organizations, particularly in leadership jobs. But awareness alone is never entirely sufficient. One also needs appropriate assets—which I have been calling sources of power and influence—to allow one to make up for the power gaps inherent in those jobs and thus to be able to act on that awareness. A central aspect of the entire career development process for people who are successful at making a real difference within modern organizations relates to the development, maintenance, and finally, relinquishment of such a power base.

Since most people begin their organizational careers with very few of these power sources—typically they have a few relevant skills and that's about all—a central challenge during the early years relates to developing the needed power base. This means accumulating massive amounts of relevant information, developing large numbers of cooperative relationships, significantly expanding personal skills, gaining control of important resources, establishing a strong track record, and getting progressively more important jobs. People who are successful in these areas then have the capacity to emerge as effective and responsible leaders in organizations. Those who naïvely or cynically focus their attention elsewhere, regardless of natural ability or effort, do not.

I

A few years ago I encountered a rather dramatic example of how differences in the focus of early career efforts can lead to major differences in outcome. The people involved, let's call them Jerry and Dave, were classmates in our MBA program.

Jerry was a bright, ambitious young MBA student. In many ways, he was typical of the people in his class. During the spring of his second year in the MBA program, he interviewed for thirty different jobs in twenty companies from nine different industries. This process eventually landed him five attractive job offers. He accepted one as a manager of a small-staff department in a large manufacturing firm. He felt this was the best offer because it sounded "like the most exciting opportunity," and because it paid the most money.

Jerry began work with great enthusiasm. He spent most of his time the first month on the job learning his department's activities and identifying its problems. In this, he was able to apply successfully his education and his intelligence. Within sixty days Jerry felt he had clearly diagnosed the group's strengths and weaknesses. Shortly thereafter he finished designing a plan of action for improving the department's performance.

Three months after starting work, Jerry announced a basic reorganization of his department, fired one of his employees, and requested permission from his boss to add one new lower-level position. He immediately received word that his boss wanted to talk to him about these plans. The subsequent discussion was a difficult one; his boss expressed concern over his plans and asked a long list of tough questions, some of which Jerry was unprepared for. As a result of the meeting, Jerry was asked to delay making any changes until his boss could study his plans more carefully. When Jerry had to announce to his employees that the changes would not be implemented immediately, his credibility with his people, which had been slowly growing up to that point, began to deteriorate.

Within the next four weeks, new problems began to emerge in the department. Jerry pointed to these problems as evidence that his changes were very much needed. But his boss was unimpressed. Instead, his boss interpreted the problems as evidence that Jerry was having difficulty with "basic" aspects of management. His boss felt that Jerry should master these "basics" before undertaking a more sophisticated reorganization of the department. Jerry disagreed and found discussing all this with his boss very frustrating. He was convinced it was important to take action quickly. But his boss continued to delay all major actions.

In his sixth month, Jerry received a scathing memo from another department manager, with a copy to his and Jerry's boss, complaining about some of the work Jerry's subordinates had recently completed. This created a minor crisis, and the series of meetings that followed absorbed much of Jerry's time for the next eight weeks. Jerry felt the memo overstated the problem and that it was sent to his boss for "political" reasons. Nevertheless, his boss took the criticisms very seriously; he saw them as more evidence that Jerry was still not mastering the basics. The "fact-finding" efforts which took place after this incident further strained relationships between Jerry and his subordinates. And morale in his department collapsed.

In his eighth month, two of his subordinates sent an anonymous complaint to Jerry's boss regarding the management of the department. This letter set in motion another series of meetings that absorbed much of Jerry's time for the next two months. By the twelfth month the situation had degenerated even further. Everyone seemed to be fighting with Jerry or with each other. By then, Jerry fully realized he was in a hopeless position ("I have trouble even getting a letter typed around here"), so he began looking for a new job in another company.

Jerry's sad early career experience stands in vivid contrast to Dave's. Dave was like Jerry in many ways, and he ended up in a very similar job. But he went about the entire process of getting that job and getting started in that job in an entirely different way.

Dave spent a considerable amount of time during the fall of his second year assessing both himself and the various types of job possibilities he knew would be available during the spring. He thought long and hard about what he really valued, what kind of people he liked and disliked, what kind of situations he tended to thrive in or have difficulty in. He also did as much research as was practical on various industries, companies, and types of entry-level jobs. By January, he had made a number of decisions regarding how he was going to focus his job search. He stood by these decisions during February and March despite a multitude of distractions that would have broadened his search. In doing so, he interviewed for twelve jobs in ten firms in three different industries, and eventually got four good job offers. After some more soul searching, he selected the one that seemed best to fit his goals, values, talents, and prior experience.

Before starting his job, Dave spent time doing some homework on his new department. In this effort he learned many things, including the chief complaint voiced by those working in the department ("not enough office space") and the most visible weakness in the department's performance ("poor planning resulting in people becoming overwhelmed with work three or four times a year"). He also took some time to develop his relationship with the company's president, who had briefly interviewed him during the recruiting process. In his final discussion with the president before starting work, he brought up what he thought were the legitimate complaints about office space and received a commitment that the department's space would be increased by about thirty percent.

Because Dave had made an impression on the president

even before starting work, the president stopped by to see Dave for a few minutes during his first week on the job. Dave's new subordinates were in awe: no one could remember the president ever coming into the department before. Dave also made the announcement about the increase in office space. His employees were elated.

In his first two months on the job, Dave concentrated on developing good relations with his subordinates, his boss, and others in other departments that he needed to depend on. For example, he sat down with each of his new subordinates and discussed their jobs; by reaching consensus regarding responsibility and authority, he created a sense of obligation in them to focus on important responsibilities and to defer to Dave's authority in certain key areas. He also devoted his attention to finding an easy way to make some progress on the planning and scheduling problem faced by the department. And he eventually did find a way. By applying some simple tools learned in graduate school in conjunction with his prior knowledge of the industry (he had worked in this industry for two years before going to graduate school), he was able to schedule work assignments so as to reduce the next peak work period significantly. Implementing the new schedule was easy, because Dave avoided changes that could have upset people.

During his tenth week, the annual "end of August chaos" didn't happen. There was still an increase in work and a decrease in the department's ability to respond quickly, but the normal peak with its associated problems disappeared. The improvement was very visible—to Dave's subordinates, to other departments, and to upper management. All were impressed. As a result of this and other victories, in less than four months on the job Dave established such a strong position that he was able to convince his boss that he needed two extra staff positions, above and beyond the budget. And he was able to get most of his subordinates to respond more systematically (and effectively) to their work.

Dave's fifth through twelfth months on the job progressed in a similar way. He continued to build good relationships with those around him. He continued to receive more resources to help him do his job. Each month he took on more difficult problems, but only after he felt he had the power to solve them. In his fifth and sixth months he developed and implemented new information and control systems. In the seventh and eighth months he reorganized the department. In his ninth month, he confronted a few personnel problems that he had been aware of since joining the firm. Two of his people simply were not performing their jobs satisfactorily. He fired one of them and got the other transferred into a more appropriate job in another department. As a result, by his tenth month, Dave had a department that was a model for others. And at the end of his first year on the job—in extreme contrast with Jerry—Dave was very successfully managing the complex milieu around him and was already starting to make a difference in his firm. He was already emerging as a young leader.

It is tempting to explain away the contrasting situations of Jerry and Dave by employing either the concept of luck (i.e., Dave was lucky and Jerry was not) or some vague notion of ability (i.e., Dave is a good manager, Jerry is not). Neither is convincing. Attributing the difference in outcomes to luck assumes no causal patterns exist that can explain those differences; in this and similar cases such a causal pattern does exist. Attributing the differences to ability requires an identification of the specific attributes involved, and that is difficult. On the surface, Jerry and Dave were very similar in intellect, social presence, general business knowledge, etc.

The most convincing pattern that helps explain the large differences in outcomes seen here relates to differences in how these two men managed to develop, or not to develop, the power sources they would need to perform really well in their first jobs. As we shall see in the discussion to follow, Jerry did very little to develop the power base he needed. Instead, he focused exclusively on business problems and decisions and solutions and opportunities. Dave paid considerable attention to those same issues, but not in the same abstract, removed, and diagnostic way. Dave's focus was implicitly guided by the question, how can I get myself into a situation where I have the necessary sources of power to be able to

correctly identify important business issues and then to provide leadership in dealing with those issues? This focus guided
his use of time, especially during the first few months on the
job. It guided the order in which he tried to tackle problems
that he identified. It even directed, as we shall see next, his
whole approach to job hunting. And all this led to a first career
experience that was much better than the norm achieved
even by very capable young people. Much better.

II

Capable young people who are entering the labor market
for the first time rarely have a clear sense of who they are,
of their limitations, and of their own real strengths and weaknesses. After being "promoted" every twelve months in school
for most of their lives, many overestimate what they can do
and where they can be both successful and happy. Others,
especially those who have not had access to good role models
at home and in school, underestimate their possibilities. Of
course, most people usually recognize that they are not as
good at history (or physics) as they are at math (or French).
But that information does not translate easily into very specific
occupational advice; it only gives the most general guidance
(e.g., "avoid accounting-type jobs"). This is unfortunate, because the development of the kind of power base that can
allow one to play a useful leadership role in modern organizations requires, first of all, that one get into an organization
and a job that match closely with one's own values and
strengths. This "fit" provides important leverage for developing that power base.[1]

In the case of Jerry and Dave, at least a part of the reason
that Dave got off to such a good start was because of a good
initial fit. Through a careful assessment of himself, of certain
industries and companies, and finally of his job offers, he entered a situation that matched his interests and capabilities
rather closely. This fit helped him relate well to the people
around him, including the company's president, which in turn
made it easier to develop cooperative relationships. The fit
made it easier to learn the substance of the job and to develop

a knowledge base, because that information was perceived as "interesting." All of this made it easier to do well quickly in the job and hence to start developing a good track record. These factors in turn helped him secure more resources, develop even more and better relationships, increase his control of good information sources, and perform even more difficult tasks well. In other words, the initial good fit helped greatly in starting the snowballing effect of developing a power base, which in turn helped him to perform his job well.

In Jerry's case there was not nearly as good an initial fit. Because of the way Jerry went about job hunting, he entered a situation that matched some of his capabilities and interests, but not many. He didn't share many of the same interests and values with the people around him, which made it more difficult to develop cooperative relationships. He didn't "love" his industry like Dave did, which made learning about it more of a chore and hence more difficult. His skills and temperament didn't match the job demands that closely either, which made it more difficult to do well quickly. Indeed, the evidence I have suggests that Jerry probably shouldn't have taken an initial job that was as demanding of good interpersonal relationships as the one he took. He didn't have any experience managing subordinates, and his awareness of the issues in managing relationships with them and others was low. Because of these factors there was a lack of fit between him and his job, and this made it difficult for him to take charge, to start the snowballing development of a power base, to provide leadership, and thus to perform well.

Over the past decade, I've seen dozens of cases where talented young people have gotten their careers off to a bad start by selecting companies and jobs which simply did not fit their capabilities and values very well. They did not do the kind of systematic assessment that Dave did. Instead, somewhat like Jerry, they looked for "good" opportunities in a more abstract sense, where "good" was usually defined in terms of what was popular in the social setting they were in. They chose job opportunities where the people and the products or services didn't really excite them, because they were seduced by the money, the glamour, the "great opportunity," or a clever selling job on the part of the employer. They also often chose jobs, as did Jerry, that were too demanding in relationship skills for them. That is, they got themselves into a social milieu which was simply over their heads.

Doing the kind of systematic assessment that Dave did is not easy by any standard. But it is possible. We have now had ten years of experience with the Career Management course at Harvard. All the evidence suggests that people can be taught to make a realistic self-assessment, to assess opportunities competently, and then to make intelligent choices. This requires more than a few hours or days of effort, but it is possible.[2]

More specifically, this kind of self-assessment demands that one systematically search for central themes in one's past and present experiences—themes that are so strong and pervasive that they say something about core values, key strengths, and important weaknesses. Competent opportunity assessment then requires that one look for industries, companies, career paths, and starting jobs that make sense in light of these themes—situations that are consistent with core values, where the strengths are really needed, and where important weaknesses are not a serious drawback.

I'm sure that I have heard a hundred times someone say, "But you can't really tell what a job (or company or industry) is like until you are actually in it for a while." Although there clearly are some things that one can only assess by participating in them over a period of time, many important questions about employment opportunities can largely be answered accurately before one ever accepts a job offer.[3] It simply requires effort and a sensitivity to the issues.

III

After getting into a situation that fits to some minimum degree, developing a power base requires, during the early career, that one use the leverage provided by the initial fit systematically to increase over time relevant personal skills, information bases, relationships, financial resources, and a track record. Doing this, in turn, requires that one take advantage of simple opportunities encountered each day for developing these sources of power. It also requires that one more strategically "invest" some power in longer-term projects on an ongoing basis in the hope of getting it back with "interest" (Dave acted in both of these ways, Jerry did neither). Finally, in terms of one's career path, it requires that one move, over time, toward positions where one can help manage some strategic contingency for the organization.

All professional, managerial, and technical people face situations each and every day where they can increase or decrease some of their power. Developing a power base in one's early career requires that one be sensitive to these opportunities, both from the point of view of gaining or enhancing sources of power and from that of not inadvertently wasting valuable power.

Some people are very good at seeing opportunities that cost them very little, but that gain them valuable information or better relationships or the like.[4] They will use a chance encounter while walking down the hall, for example, to have a brief chat with someone and, in that brief encounter, find ways of both asking a few relevant questions to get some information they need, and of sincerely complimenting the person on some job well done, thus enhancing their relationship. They are equally sensitive to opportunities for increasing their control over needed financial resources, for building relationships based on an obligation by helping people with their jobs, and so on. Dave was sensitive to these kinds of opportunities, and he invested a lot of his time in them during the first month or two. Jerry did not.

Furthermore, in a more strategic sense, developing power requires that one take risks with one's power and invest it, much like entrepreneurs invest money.[5] That is, one needs to use relationships, personal skills, information, and financial resources to try to achieve something important for one's organization, in the hopes of thus gaining an enhanced track record, a promotion to a more powerful position, increased skills, and perhaps stronger relationships with more powerful mentors. These new resources can then be used to build more and better relationships and to gain more and better information, which can then be invested along with other power sources in some new project, in the hopes once again of getting even more in return. Effective leaders, during their early careers, tend to be very good at this strategic investment activity.

Dave was. From day one, he looked for important opportunities that he could "afford"—that is, business problems that he had the power to solve. Jerry made poor investments, in a way that is very typical of many capable young people. He tackled what he perceived to be the most important problem first, despite the fact that he did not have the power to be able to deal with it effectively. In the process, he lost rather than gained power, and he put himself in a position where it was even more difficult to get anything important done.

A very typical example of a young person who, like Dave, was skilled at this investment activity, can be seen in the case of the young man who, after being employed for about three years in one firm, sought and obtained a transfer into an area that he had learned was critical to the company's five-year growth plans. He was put in charge of a construction project, where he used all the resources he had to finish the project one day ahead of schedule. This cost him a significant investment of power but led directly to a large increase in his professional reputation, the development of a strong mentor relationship with a vice-president, and a promotion in the same area. Because of the latter, he gained more formal authority, more responsibilities, more tangible assets, and the control of some new information channels. He quickly used these additional resources to develop even more power. For example, he used his new mentor relationship to help turn competitive relationships with some of his peers into more cooperative relationships, because they felt more dependent on him due to his "in" with top management. He then used this additional power to exceed his financial and other objectives for the year. This accomplishment led to still another promotion.

A key part of this power-development strategy usually involves (as it did in this case) moving toward projects or jobs or departments that are strategically important to the organization.[6] Positions in those areas allow one to control particularly important contingencies for the firm, and this gives one power. In an industry where selling is particularly important, this might mean moving into and up the sales hierarchy. In a firm where R&D is the key to its future plans, this might involve moving into and up the R&D ladder.

Consider, for example, the young woman who took a low-level managerial job at a hospital in Philadelphia. In 1970 she requested and obtained a transfer to a similar job in a different part of the hospital. The good track record she had established during her first year allowed her to ask for and seriously be considered for this move. But she received the transfer mainly because no one comparable wanted the job. Her request for the transfer was based on an analysis of a number of important changes that were occurring then. She recognized that changes within the medical profession and in federal laws were going to make a considerable amount of money available to one relatively obscure department in the hospital. So when the manager of that department was promoted, she requested that job. And her analysis proved to be correct. As a result, she was able to increase that department's budget over a three-year period by over 2,000 percent. That, in turn, brought her attention and prestige which, a few years later, led to a promotion into one of the key management jobs in the hospital. Today, her dream of being able to play a significant leadership role in a health care organization has become a reality.

As these last two cases suggest, people who are successful at developing power during their early careers establish a "success syndrome" in which, year after year, they find ways to increase their power-related personal skills, their cooperative relationships with others, the amount of relevant information they process, the resources they command, their track records, and the size of their jobs. In this way, they propel themselves into leadership positions that, although difficult, are manageable.[7]

An examination of the careers of dozens of successful businesspeople shows this basic pattern again and again. John Opel, the chairman of IBM, is typical in this regard. Opel joined IBM early in his career and stayed there (a power base usually doesn't move well when you change companies). He moved through a wide variety of jobs, which exposed him to most of the business and most of the key people (he didn't just get promoted up a narrow hierarchy). His early successes led to a job in 1959 as an assistant to Chief Executive Officer Thomas Watson, Jr. This mentor relationship, his knowledge and relationship base, and his track record and reputation, helped him perform well in more and more difficult, and more and more strategically important assignments. This led to his appointment as president in 1974, and as CEO in 1981. And this career path equipped him with the power base needed to perform these jobs very effectively.

Everyone between the ages of twenty and forty could probably profit by periodically examining their own careers in terms of the development of a power base and a success syndrome. This means considering questions such as these:

- Over the past twelve months, how much have I really learned about the products or services, the markets, the technologies, and the people with whom I deal? How does this increase in my relevant knowledge compare to what I learned last year? The year before that?
- In the past year, how many new people have I gotten to know at work? How many people have I strengthened or improved my relationship with? Have I alienated anyone?
- What new skills have I developed in the past year? Are my analytic skills and judgment better in certain areas? How about my interpersonal skills?
- What have I added to my track record in the past twelve months? If I were to update last year's resume, what would I add?
- Is my reputation as good or better than it was a year ago? If not, why not? Is it because my track record doesn't look as good? Or is it because I haven't done enough to bring my good track record to the attention of others?

Even people who do not aspire to positions of considerable responsibility could benefit by reflecting on these questions.

Lower-level managerial, professional, and technical jobs, if they are to be performed well, almost always require some power beyond the authority that automatically comes with the job. And power rarely comes to or is maintained by someone who is oblivious to it.

IV

There are a number of reasons why capable individuals, even those that get off to a good start in their careers, still do not develop and maintain the kind of power sources and success syndrome just described. Perhaps the most important one is this: Oblivious to the issues just described, they pay attention to the wrong indices in measuring their career progress and then make bad choices, which get them into jobs that are over their heads. That, in turn, leads to ineffective performance, occasionally to the misuse of power, and virtually always to a destruction of their "success syndrome."

There is a strong tendency among capable young people to focus on income and promotions as the most appropriate measures of career progress, even in the short run. The rule of thumb used is simple: the faster income goes up and the more promotions one gets, the better. This guiding principle leads people not to pay enough attention to developing relationships, knowledge, a track record, skills, their reputations, etc. As a result, they often don't systematically build the power base they need, or they unintentionally undermine it. (Some very talented people I have known have severely wounded themselves by gaining reputations as young manipulative hotshots, who only care about their own careers.) Even worse, this tendency leads them to seek and accept big promotions or more lucrative salaries in other firms, despite the fact that they simply do not have the power sources needed to perform well in those new jobs.

I encountered a good example of this problem a few years ago in a financial services organization. A manager in his middle thirties was given a lateral transfer because his new boss was not satisfied with his performance. Neither was the manager himself, although he thought that "under the circumstances," he had done a pretty good job. On the surface, it is difficult to understand why this person did not perform better in that job. He was very bright, certainly brighter than the average manager or professional in the firm. He had an MBA degree, knew a lot about management, and even occasionally taught courses at a local business school. He had been quite successful in his early career at his company; he was one of the youngest people ever to be put in charge of a branch office, and when he was promoted into the "troublesome" job, he was about the youngest vice-president in the firm. He began the job pretty much knowing what was wrong with the area for which he was made responsible. He knew, more or less, what he needed to do. But he never was able to implement his basic agenda; he was never able to provide leadership. Indeed, he spent most of his three-year tenure in this job simply "coping," "fighting fires," and trying to "keep his head above water."

A closer examination of this situation—an examination which focuses on the dependence inherent in the job, the power inherent in the job, and the power the man was able to bring with him to the job—offers an explanation as to why this happened. First of all, the job itself had a relatively high power gap, both because of a lot of complex dependencies, and because of the relatively small amount of power inherent in the job. The complex dependence was created by the significant scope of the job's responsibilities (numerous products and markets), the large number of people who were relevant, new information-processing technologies, a highly specialized organizational structure (which required that the job depend on nearly a dozen different staff groups that did not report to the job), a tall management hierarchy (despite its importance, the job reported four levels below the chairman), and still other factors. But at the same time, the job provided the incumbent with relatively little real power. Although he did have some hiring, firing, promoting, and rewarding authority over the people who reported to him, these rights were moderated by a variety of organizational "policies." The resources that came with the job were highly limited. Because this part of the firm had not been very profitable, there had been great pressure to reduce its budget, and "slack" was virtually nonexistent. Furthermore, because this part of the firm had not been growing, it had not attracted the better employees. When the manager took over the job, a number of his people were clearly not performing very well. Finally, his job reported to the least powerful and least respected member of top management.

Coping effectively with this type of situation requires that the jobholder bring considerable assets to the job. The manager in this case did not, despite his abilities and good track record, primarily because he got the job by means of a very big promotion. In one step, he went from having about a dozen subordinates to having nearly six hundred. Almost overnight the size of his universe expanded by a factor of twenty or more. Suddenly, he was responsible for people he had not even met and operating units in which he had never worked. So, he entered the job without having a lot of relevant product, market, and technological information, without having developed some of the skills needed for dealing with large groups of subordinates (especially delegation skills), without having relationships with most of the people below or above him who were now important, and with no track record in a number of the areas for which he was now responsible. Without these important sources of power, he was never able to get control of the many complex dependencies or to find enough time to develop the needed power. And as a result, a talented young man who had performed excellently in previous jobs, performed at only a "fair" level, thus damaging his track record and reputation.

A more extreme example can be seen in John Dean's book, *Blind Ambition.*[8] In 1970, at the age of thirty-two, Dean was offered "the opportunity of a lifetime": the President of the United States wanted him to accept a job in the White House as counsel to the President. Without a great deal of thought, Dean accepted what amounted to a huge promotion (at the time he was working as a lawyer in the Justice Department), despite the fact that (1) he really didn't know anybody in the White House, (2) he didn't know that many people in Washington, since he had only recently started working for the federal government, (3) he did not know much about the job of counsel to the President or the issues confronting someone in that job, (4) he had little legal experience at all, (5) he had established little if any track record in his short tenure with the government, and (6) the information he did have about the White House suggested it was a place where people were "drained from long hours of pressure" and where "able men are reduced to gophers and errand boys, breaking their necks whenever one of the President's top aides had a whim." He took the job because it was "too great a chance to be turned down."

Within the following two-and-a-half years, Dean found himself hopelessly entangled in what came to be called "Watergate." He ended up doing things that, even he subsequently admitted, were illegal and immoral. He was made a scapegoat by a group of people far more powerful than he was. His professional reputation was ruined. And he ended up in jail!

Much less extreme, but nevertheless similar, examples of power misuse by young managers and professionals can be found commonly in organizations. Some people misuse their power by building and protecting little kingdoms within their organizations. Others develop the habit of always arriving late to meetings with their subordinates, thus continually wasting their time, just to remind them who is the boss. And still other managers, especially those supervising routine functions, will sometimes selectively enforce or ignore work rules in order to gain power over others, regardless of the negative organizational consequences. In some of these cases, I do not doubt that individual integrity is the central issue. But, in a lot of others, I suspect the key factor relates to relative powerlessness caused by someone being promoted into a job that was simply over his or her head.

V

An awareness of the pitfalls just described can be very valuable to people early in their careers. But there is only so much individuals can do by themselves. After that they need help.

There are many things that organizations can do to help young people develop adequate power bases. As Yale sociologist Rosabeth Kanter notes in her book *The Change Masters,* firms can:

- Make nonconfidential information about the business and the organization more widely available to people.
- Encourage and provide settings for relationship development.
- Provide vehicles for reputation building.
- Explicitly encourage mentoring processes.

Unfortunately, as Kanter points out, most firms do far less than they should in all four of these areas.

The issue of mentors is particularly important. It seems to be more and more widely recognized these days that mentors, sponsors, coaches, and role-models can play an especially important role in helping young people during their early careers. However, in thinking about mentors, coaches, etc., we have a tendency to see them as "teachers." And clearly an important part of what they do is teach. But really to appreciate the special role these people can play, it helps greatly to consider the issue from a power and influence perspective.

Effective mentors are usually effective because they are powerful. They have a wealth of useful information about their firms and industries and functions. They have lots of good contacts and friendships with others. They have strong track records and personal skills. They are often in important jobs that control substantial resources. And this strong power base enables them to play an important mentoring role.

Indeed, to get talented young people into jobs that truly fit them, to keep them from being promoted too quickly (or too slowly), to make sure they are not inadvertently wounded in some power struggle among more senior people—all this requires considerable power. It is not a coincidence that John Dean had no real mentor at the White House, that the young manager in the financial services organization had no real mentor in the top management of his firm, or that Jerry was also mentorless in his first job after graduate school.

Furthermore, helping junior people develop their own power bases requires power on the part of the "helper." It is most difficult to help a young person develop useful relationships unless you have those relationships yourself. A mentor cannot provide someone with key information or financial resources unless he or she already has control of those power sources. And you normally cannot help another develop key skills and abilities in any particular area unless you already possess those skills yourself.

Virtually all of the successful and effective executives I have known have had two or more of these kinds of relationships early in their careers. Some have had upwards of a dozen people whom they were able to rely on for different needs— some provided important contacts, others gave key information in specific areas, and still others taught them certain valued skills.

Although almost all large corporations, and many small ones too, acknowledge the importance of mentoring, coaching, sponsoring, and role-modeling for the development of their next generation of leaders, few seem to do a very good job in this regard. All too often, this activity is given a low priority by busy executives, and the young are left to fend for themselves. And all too often, young and talented people end up with no real mentors, or an overreliance on just one, which can be dangerous. By depending too much on one person alone, an individual becomes vulnerable to everybody and everything to which the other person is vulnerable. And when conflict arises between the mentor and the protégé— which is almost inevitable some of the time—the protégé is left in a very weak position.

(The problem caused by overreliance on a single mentor is dramatically shown in the Bill Agee-Mary Cunningham situation at Bendix a few years ago. Despite the fact that Ms. Cunningham had a very strong mentorlike relationship with the most powerful person in the company (Agee was the chief executive officer), because she had no other sponsor-like relationships in the firm and no other real power base, she was left in a vulnerable position. And sure enough, when she came under fire from others, not even Agee, who was also being attacked by those upset with his leadership of the company, could save her job.)

Because of a variety of potential problems, it is absolutely necessary for people to pay explicit attention to the mentor issue, especially during their twenties and early thirties. Periodically reflecting on the following questions can help in this regard:

- With whom do I currently have a mentor-like relationship? What role does each of these people play in my development? How well do they play their roles?
- If I don't have many mentors, or the right mix of people, or powerful enough people, why is this? Does the nature of my job simply not make me very visible to potential mentors? Is my track record or reputation not strong enough to attract mentors? Do I have a tendency not to seek out mentors, or to ignore their offers of help? Or am I simply in an environment in which few potential mentors exist?

VI

One of the most widely quoted phrases in the English language is, "Power corrupts, and absolute power corrupts absolutely." This reflects our general inclination to be concerned about people getting too much power.[9] We focus on this possibility of an excess of power because we think it invariably leads to its misuse. This is truly ironic, since one of the biggest problems in modern organizations is related not to an excess of power, but to the fact that too many people have too little power,[10] especially people in leadership jobs. And this situation is not going to change until we do a better job of helping people manage their careers, especially during the early stages. As the chapter has suggested, this means doing a better job of:

1. Getting young people into contexts that fit their interests, values, skills, and weaknesses.
2. Helping them to use the leverage provided by that fit

to develop relationships, knowledge, skills, track record, etc., on the job.

3. Teaching them how to select appropriate problems and priorities, so that they invest this power wisely, avoid tackling issues they cannot resolve, and then develop the success syndrome that leads to an ever-expanding power base.

4. Watching out that they do not pay attention only to pay raises and promotions as indices of career progress, but instead monitor more appropriate measures of power growth.

5. Making sure that their speed of movement is neither too fast nor too slow, so as not to undermine their success syndrome.

6. Helping them to develop one particularly important source of power—relationships to mentors, coaches, sponsors, and the like.

Helping people to do all this well is not easy. But it is doable. And in a society that will require more and more capable leadership in the future, it is a necessity.

CHAPTER 8

MID-CAREER
Using Power Without Abusing It

By the time they have reached middle age, those people who have been successful at developing a strong power base in their early careers usually wield considerable influence. Operating out of major leadership jobs, their actions affect the lives of thousands, sometimes millions, of people. They are, by most definitions, important; they have "made it."

There is a tendency among many people to think that, for those who have "made it," power problems no longer exist. The struggles they experienced on the way up are over. They have arrived. They are now in control.

Nothing could be further from the truth.

I

In the spring of 1977, the sixty-two-year-old chief executive officer of a financial services company was elected chairman of the board and the forty-eight-year-old vice-president of finance was named as his successor. The announcement of this change was received well, although many people inside the firm were surprised; they had assumed the marketing vice-president would get the CEO's job.

Shortly after starting his job, the new CEO tried to neutralize what he saw as a potential problem. He fully realized that the marketing vice-president had wanted the CEO's job very much and was undoubtedly quite disappointed, since at sixty he was probably too old to get another shot at the job. The new CEO sensed that these feelings could lead his vice-president, if only subconsciously, to be less cooperative than the CEO needed him to be. The CEO considered a number of options to reduce the chances of this problem ever developing and had a few exploratory chats with his vice-president about the possibility of top jobs in other firms. Those discussions led to no action, however, and because the CEO was so busy getting up to speed in his new job, he followed through on none of his other ideas. If this really developed into a problem, he thought to himself, he could deal with it then.

Nine months later, it became clear that the CEO did have a problem with his vice-president. Although there was never anything very blatant, his top marketing officer was just not cooperating like the others on his team. All the time this man seemed to be fighting him in small and subtle ways. He tried a few times to talk to his vice-president about it, but the discussions were awkward and never seemed to accomplish anything. He considered bringing the subject up with the chairman or with the other vice-presidents, but since he could not point to concrete evidence that there was a problem, he did not.

After a few more months, since the situation had not improved, the CEO decided that his ability to perform his job to his and his boss's satisfaction was being seriously impaired. To design and implement successful new strategies to cope with an increasingly competitive business environment, he knew he needed the complete support of all his vice-presidents. So he reluctantly decided to force his vice-president of marketing either out of the company or into a less important job. But as he went about planning this action, he began to encounter some disturbing evidence about how powerful his marketing vice-president was, how strongly he could resist efforts to move him out, and how much damage he could inflict on the company if he wanted.

Marketing and sales were generally recognized as the keys to success in this firm's industry, and the firm was known to have an excellent sales force. A loss of a significant number of salespeople, or even a lot of turmoil in the department, could have a serious effect on the firm's performance. The CEO was well aware of these facts, and he also knew that the marketing vice-president had been with the firm for twenty-five years and had personally hired many of the salespeople. But what he didn't know was just how popular the vice-president was with the sales force, and just how strong his relationships were to thirty or forty of the biggest producers. As new evidence made this clear to him, he came to realize that the option of forcing the vice-president out, an option he assumed was viable when he stopped pursuing his early discussions with the vice-president about outside opportunities, was really not viable.

So one year into his new job, the CEO found himself in the incredibly frustrating position of having a key dependency who was very much inclined to resist full cooperation and who was powerful enough to get away with it.

We often think that as one rises in an organization and becomes more powerful, the problems caused by diversity and interdependence go away, or at least become easier to handle. As this example suggests, they do not disappear, and they do not become trivial. Quite the contrary, the power gaps tend to grow larger as one goes up the hierarchy, and the problems associated with the diverse yet interdependent social milieu in complex organizations often peak in top-level jobs. Somewhat ironically, "success" means having the privilege to deal with the most complex problems in an environment where mistakes can not only be damaging personally, but can also adversely affect thousands of other people.

Thirty years ago, a relatively small number of people had to deal with this reality. The powerful elite in business and government could be identified and actually counted. Today, with far more big leadership jobs in existence, these problems affect thousands and thousands of upper-level managers and executives. And tomorrow even more of us will probably be affected. How well we will be able to deal with all this will depend on how well we come to grips with the challenges presented in these highly complex leadership jobs. And on how well we learn to respond to these challenges. We still have a lot to learn.

II

The situation facing someone in a significant leadership role in a modern organization is similar in many ways to the situation facing all managers, professionals, and technical specialists. That is, such a person is made dependent on a diverse group of bosses (even if he is a CEO, there is a board), subordinates, peers, and outsiders, some of whom are also interdependent in complex ways. In return, he or she is given some formal resources and some formal authority over those who are subordinates. But in top jobs, because of their very nature, the number of relevant relationships, the extent of the diversity among those people, and the degree of interdependence is simply much greater than in the typical managerial, professional, or technical job. And even taking into account the considerable power that comes with these jobs, the power gap is still much larger than in lower-level jobs.

For example, a typical middle-aged executive in a general management job will have the following responsibilities: [1]

1. Long run—setting some or all of the basic goals, directions, and priorities for an organization, including deciding what business or businesses to be in, and how to secure key resources.
2. Medium run—allocating resources effectively to that business or those businesses so as to achieve long-run goals.
3. Short run—the efficient use of the human, financial, and material resources employed in that business or those businesses, including some profit responsibility.

These responsibilities, in the context of a typical moderate-sized organization, make a general manager dependent in nontrivial ways on from one to ten thousand people, many of them subordinates of subordinates, and most of the rest outsiders (customers, suppliers, union officials, etc.). This is mind-boggling when you consider that most people spend their first twenty or thirty years of life in environments where the number of relevant others that must be depended upon is perhaps two or three dozen. It is no wonder that many people cannot even conceive of what it would be like to be dependent on thousands of others.

A simple example helps illustrate the point. If a general manager who has 5,000 dependencies associated with his job wanted to see each of these people individually just once a month and for only fifteen minutes each, and if he were willing to allocate all except two hours a day to accomplish this task, and if to save time he could get all of them to come to him (this is unrealistic, but for this example it simplifies things), then how long would his typical workday need to be? If you guessed more than twenty-four hours, you're on the right track. The answer is well over fifty hours long!

Some people will discount this kind of example because they believe that although a general manager may operate in a universe in which thousands of people are relevant, he or she really isn't very dependent on more than a dozen, or at most a hundred of them. Although the rest may play some small part, they can't significantly affect the general manager's performance. People with these beliefs would benefit from talking to the Chase Manhattan executives who recently had to cope with the "Drysdale" affair. These are the few Chase general managers who, as a part of their 10,000- to 100,000-person "universes," had 9 individuals, buried layers below them in the hierarchy, people who were located (literally) in a third subbasement at Chase headquarters, who somehow managed to create a situation which cost the bank a $135 million after-tax write-off and put, as the *Wall Street Journal* put it, "an ugly pimple on its reputation." [2]

Further complicating the situation greatly is the enormous diversity among the people on whom a top executive may be dependent. A typical general manager must cope simultaneously with strong pressures from financial markets to produce a growing and predictable income stream on a quarterly basis and with pressures from his or her R&D, product development, and organizational development people to maintain a certain steady level of funding for important longer-run projects, regardless of the impact on short-run earnings. He or she must deal with complaints from important customers or clients who want faster service or a better price or whatever and, at the same time, with legitimate concerns from his or her manufacturing and sales executives who have to meet budgets and serve still other customers. He or she must simultaneously cope with senior managers who are feeling threatened by aggressive and upwardly mobile younger managers, and with those same junior managers who feel their careers are being blocked by an "over-the-hill gang." The list of serious and ongoing conflicts caused by diversity is a long one.

Both the naïve and the cynical tend to underestimate the diversity involved and the difficulty of dealing with it. They see the job in more unidimensional terms, believing that "maximizing shareholder wealth," or "maximizing sales," or some similar objective, is key. They simply refuse to see that there are multiple legitimate constituencies or stakeholders involved and that management at this level involves the extremely difficult but important task of finding ways to satisfy all legitimate claims.[3]

Of course, to help cope with the situation, a typical general manager is given considerable power. The job provides resources and formal authority. But even these assets, in some ways, make the job more difficult, because with them come serious ethical and moral responsibilities. The decisions made by a typical general manager can affect thousands, even millions of people, now and in the future. Hence, the job demands that these decisions be made with great care. Yet because of the large number of people involved, the sometimes conflicting interests of those people, and the many uncertainties introduced by complex technologies and the like, figuring out what the "right" decision is can be incredibly difficult.

Take, for example, the situation which once confronted

Randolph Barton, the president of Parker Brothers.[4] Now owned by General Mills, the company is a respected century-old maker of games and toys, including *Monopoly*. In 1977, the firm introduced a new product called the *Riviton Construction Toy*, which quickly became very popular, selling nearly half a million sets that year at close to twenty dollars each. For a company whose total yearly revenues were in the $100 million range, this was a huge success.

On April 4, 1978, Mr. Barton received a telephone call from the Toy Manufacturers of America, a trade association, informing him that approximately three months earlier, an eight-year-old boy from Menomonee Falls, Wisconsin, had suffocated because a *Riviton* rivet had lodged in his left lung. Apparently, the boy was playing soft ball with his brother in a hallway in their home while he had a rivet in his mouth. Suddenly he began to choke, and after mouth-to-mouth resuscitation efforts by the boy's parents failed, he was dead on arrival at the hospital. Subsequently, the Federal Consumer Product Safety Commission conducted an investigation of the incident and recommended that no action be taken against Parker Brothers. Armed with the knowledge that the toy met all voluntary (industry) and government standards for product safety, and that the death clearly occurred because of product misuse, Barton decided to take no special action at the time.

On Thursday, November 16, 1978, Barton received a telephone call from a New Jersey newspaper reporter who informed him that a nine-year-old boy in Kearney, New Jersey, had suffocated on a *Riviton* rivet. It took Barton until the following Monday to confirm the report and get the details. As in the first death, the rivet lodged itself in the youngster's lung.

Once again Barton had to make a decision. The facts were these: On the one hand, both deaths were clearly the result of product misuse; the toy still met and exceeded all safety standards; Barton was under no pressure (yet) from the government to do anything; and any action at this point could cost a lot of money (a total recall, for example, would wipe out the firm's entire profits for the year, jeopardize other new product development, strain the company's relationship with

General Mills, and probably affect employee bonuses and raises). But on the other hand, other children's lives and the reputation of the company were also at stake.

The example may sound somewhat unusual but, in reality, situations far more complex than this one occur every year; the case of Procter & Gamble and the Rely tampon is a good example.[5] Less dramatic cases undoubtedly occur all the time. In such cases, it would be nice if the people involved could calmly gather data and take their time in making a decision. But the pressures and stakes rarely make that possible. One must act quickly and without perfect information. And the diverse pressures involved can—to paraphrase the title from Chapter 4 of J. Patrick Wright's book on General Motors[6]— easily lead "moral men to make immoral decisions."

(Barton, by the way, decided that in his case lives and corporate reputation were more important. He ordered a complete product recall.)

III

Because of the nature of the situation facing successful executives at midlife, despite the fact that such people are, in an absolute sense, very powerful, they can still find themselves in the incredibly frustrating position of not being powerful enough to execute their duties in an effective and responsible way, and to provide the leadership that is needed. Like the new president of the financial services organization, even someone with all of the resources and authority associated with a CEO's job can still lack enough clout to solve a centrally important problem.

This type of rather basic power problem occurs for a number of reasons. Sometimes, especially in the early career stage, people are promoted into top jobs that are simply over their heads. When this happens, poor performance is almost inevitable, and the misuse of power is common.

Take, for example, the case of a moderately small manufacturing firm that was once the leader in its industry. When I encountered it in 1974, it had fallen upon hard times. Upon examination, I found that the deterioration in the firm's health occurred primarily during the tenure of a previous, now deceased, president. This person was a sales executive who had been named president of the company by the founder of the company when the founder retired. The founder was childless and had looked upon this man as a son. Although it is hard to reconstruct the exact situation when the sales executive took over this job, the evidence suggests that, somewhat like the young manager in the financial services organization described in the last chapter, he got in considerably over his head. He had been in sales all his life, had never had to deal with a more general management job, had never had to deal with hundreds of employees as subordinates, had never had to deal with manufacturing or accounting technologies, and so on. To cope, he informally reorganized the company so that, instead of having six vice-presidents report to him, he had no less than twenty-two people report directly to him, most of them subordinates of the six vice-presidents. Although this move eventually created great problems for the firm, for a few years it helped him avoid being highly dependent on his two key vice-presidents (for marketing and manufacturing). He also began to abandon growth and profitability goals, despite the fact that profit margins were slipping. In those and still other ways, he essentially misused the power of his office to reduce his job-related dependencies to the point where he could barely manage them. And in the process, over a six-year period, he severely wounded the firm.

Even people who have been extraordinarily successful, effective, and responsible in their early careers are vulnerable to this problem. John DeLorean is a perfect case in point.[7] During John's first fifteen years at GM, he was both an enormously effective manager (by most accounts) and an extremely successful one. But later, with his dream of DeLorean Motorcar Company collapsing all around him, he appears to have taken steps which many people would consider a clear abuse of his power.

To some degree, this type of problem occurs because it is tough for a successful and ambitious person to say, in essence: "No thank you. I don't think I am really prepared yet to found a company," or "I don't think I'm ready to become president of my current firm." Indeed, highly competent and successful executives, after years and years of a "success syndrome," often develop the attitude of "I can do anything." [8] (DeLorean certainly seems to have believed that.) And that sometimes gets them into trouble at the peak of their careers, especially when the "anything" means running a big company for which they have never worked, in an industry that is new to them.

An excellent example of this phenomenon can be seen in the case of Roy Ash.[9] In his early career, Ash helped build Litton Industries into what has been called "one of the brightest stars in the U.S. business scene." He then went to Washington and created the idea of an Office of Management and Budget. After Washington, Ash spent some time managing his personal finances and trying to write a book; then he decided he wanted to run something again. That something turned out to be what was then called Addressograph-Multigraph (now AM International).

AM was a Cleveland-based producer of office machines, with revenues in the mid-1970s of around $600 million a year. Because its once leading line of machines was being challenged by newer rivals like Xerox, IBM, and Eastman-Kodak, at least some of its directors were concerned that the firm needed "a change of direction." One of them talked to an investment banker who later talked to Ash. After careful examination of the numbers, Ash concluded that the firm offered a great opportunity for him. So he bought 300,000 shares of AM stock, at a cost of $2.7 million, and accepted an offer from the board to take over as chief executive officer.

Ash began his job at AM with about as much going for him as is possible for someone moving into a new company and industry at a high level. He had the CEO job. He was the largest stockholder. He arrived with an excellent reputation. He is a very bright individual, and after his years at Litton and in Washington, he brought with him great experience and skill.

Ash quickly identified some of the firm's basic problems and launched into his work in a nearly textbook-perfect way.

Indeed, a *Fortune* article written about a year and a half after he took over AM is positively laudatory. His basic approach to the challenge at AM was so sound that a friend of mine at McKinsey, the consulting firm, used to give the article to his clients who were embarking on large organizational change efforts. I even used it once, for the same reason, in a course at Harvard.

The *Fortune* article was written in early 1978. In early 1981, AM's board fired Roy Ash. It seems that during Ash's tenure, sales went up modestly, from $666 million in 1978 to $857 million in 1981. But meager profits of $21 million in 1978, dropped to $12 million in 1979, $6 million in 1980, and to a huge loss of $245 million in 1981. Meanwhile debt soared from $92 million to $250 million, and equity sank from $218 million down to $14 million.

A recent postmortem of Ash's time at AM in *Business Week* doesn't criticize his basic strategy. People agree that it was right "on target." One of the firm's veteran managers is quoted as saying that "you can't fault the prior management for the basic direction. But you can fault them for execution. That's what caused the company to go to hell."

Despite all the assets Roy Ash brought with him to AM, he lacked two that are essential for successful execution: detailed knowledge of the products, technologies, markets, and people involved and good cooperative relationships with the relevant players. For a company the size of AM, which is not really very large by today's standards, that's a lot of information and a lot of people. Without these power sources, the effective execution of major changes is almost impossible. And developing them from scratch, in anything larger than a relatively small firm, requires a long time. Indeed, this is one of the key reasons why there is so little executive mobility among firms at high levels[10] (despite the impression to the contrary that we sometimes get from the business press).

IV

Power problems also regularly occur among successful executives who have clearly not gotten into jobs that are over their heads. The complex situations they are in produce both strategic choice and implementation traps that are easy to fall into.

Almost all executives in all organizations seek steady growth as one of their most central objectives. They do so because a constantly increasing stream of resources makes it much easier to manage their large and diverse set of relationships. Growth means more job opportunities, which makes it easier to manage relationships with employees. Growth means the possibility of greater dividends and higher stock prices, making it easier to manage relationships with stockholders. Growth means more supplies of all types must be purchased or leased, making it easier to deal with suppliers and banks.

Relatively young organizations tend to achieve growth by simply selling their products or services to a larger and larger market. But after a while, all markets mature, and growth can only come at the expense of competitors. Fighting it out for a larger share of a stable market is an extremely difficult and risky way to try to grow. So some form of diversification, either through internal development or by acquisition, is required. That is, the company must take on new products or services.

Diversification always increases diversity and interdependence and complicates top-level jobs. Too much diversification too fast can turn a set of jobs for which the incumbents were more than qualified into jobs which are clearly over their heads. But because diversification, especially via acquisition, pushes up sales and profits, it may take a number of years before this problem becomes obvious to people.

It is not by chance that the record, in general, for companies that have chosen extreme diversification—so-called conglomerates—is not nearly as good as for those who chose less extreme forms.[11] Nor is it accidental that many of the firms that got caught up in the extreme diversification craze during the late 1960s and early 1970s are now retrenching.

RCA, in many ways, offers a good example of this situation.[12] In 1966, when General David Sarnoff retired after building RCA into a billion dollar corporation, the firm was

in a number of related electronic businesses. And it was finan-
cially healthy. Fifteen years later, after RCA had acquired
food, real estate, car rental, publishing, financial, and furniture
businesses—and then sold most of them—the firm's profitability as a percent of sales was a mere ten percent of what it
had been in 1966! Furthermore, management turnover was
high, and the environment was reported to be "highly politi-
cized."

If the stage for such "strategic choice traps" is set by needs
for steady growth, then it is the changing environment that
most firms operate in that sets the stage for the "implementation trap." Very few organizations today operate in stable
environments. Competitors bring out new products or offer
new services. Technological developments make existing
products or manufacturing processes obsolete. Governmental
legislation changes the rules which must be obeyed. Raw material cartels form or disband, drastically changing the price
of supplies. Interest rates and stock prices fluctuate, shifting
the cost of financing and the relative advantage of various
forms of financing.

Managing these external relationships when the changes
are large almost always requires producing some appropriate
adaptive change inside the organization. Those internal
changes, in turn, can easily run into resistance, followed by
a power struggle and a drop in the organization's performance, unless the top management handles the change process very skillfully.[13]

A typical example would be the case of a medium-sized
high-tech firm that was the leader in its field during the early
1960s.[14] The nature of its business began to shift, both in terms
of its primary customer (from the Navy to the Air Force),
and in terms of the nature of the work (from high tech to
very high tech). To win a very important contract in 1963,
the president of the firm agreed to an Air Force request,
which was virtually a demand, that the firm manage the contract not with its traditional functional organization, but with
the addition of a program office. The Air Force felt that such
an organizational change was necessary to get the coordina-

tion and control needed in this and future advanced development programs.

When work started on this new contract, the president did establish a program office, although he did it over the strong objections of his vice-presidents for engineering and manufacturing. And when the person in the program office, who was appointed manager of this new contract, tried to set up his organization and do his job, he found that most of the engineering managers strongly resisted all his efforts. The vice-president for engineering was even quoted at one point saying, "Technical integration has always been performed by the engineering department, and as far as I'm concerned, always will be. . . . I think your proposed provision that all customer contact be conducted through the program office is unnecessary and unworkable."

In the ensuing struggle between the new program office and the old functional departments, especially engineering, the company began to miss deadlines and go over cost. The Air Force grew increasingly upset. And by November 1964, the firm found itself in the position of being 30 percent over cost, four months behind schedule, and highly criticized by its most promising future customer.

This kind of adaptation problem can be found with great frequency today. Indeed, a colleague of mine at Stanford, Professor Jeff Pfeffer, has said that when he teaches in executive education programs the case on which this incident is based, a case called Federal Radar Corporation (a disguised name), it is typical for half the audience to be convinced that the situation is based on some incident that occurred in their own firms!

Adaptation problems and implementation traps are avoidable, but this requires strong leadership in the form of forward thinking, a keen sensitivity to what changes will be needed in the future, a good diagnosis of when resistance is likely and the reasons for it, and a carefully thought-out and implemented plan for reducing or overcoming the resistance.

A good example in this regard would be actions taken in the mid-1950s by executives at Stop & Shop, a Boston-based supermarket chain, to try to change certain aspects of the behavior of its managerial work force.[15] A variety of changes in their industry since World War II, along with their own growth, had led to an erosion in Stop & Shop's operating margins. The executives involved concluded that the only way to stop this erosion was to "decentralize" certain aspects of decision making. Such decentralization required substantial changes in how a number of layers of management would behave. Recognizing that there were a lot of people involved, and that for many of the older employees the changes would not come easily, the management took all of the following formal and informal steps to minimize and overcome resistance to the changes:

1. They changed the formal structure of the firm, creating, among other things, a new and more powerful job lower down in the hierarchy than existed before (the store manager).
2. They made a number of personnel changes. For example, they put those executives who had studied this problem and designed the changes into key positions where they would have responsibility for actually providing the leadership needed to implement the changes.
3. They installed a number of new information and control systems to supply payroll, inventory, and other data on a regular basis to managers lower in the organization.
4. They set up training programs for those managers most affected by the changes.
5. They instituted a number of new group meetings, again for those managers most affected by the changes. These meetings were held on a regular basis as a vehicle for helping the managers adjust to the changes and, eventually, as a source of peer pressure on those managers who were resisting the changes.

These measures, carefully implemented and monitored by the top management team, helped the firm to adapt successfully to changes in their industry and to their own growth. Their margins, which had been falling for at least five years, began to rise and continued to go up for a number of years.

V

Coping with the situation facing a successful executive in an effective and responsible way requires great awareness and skill in dealing with all three of the types of organizational relationships discussed in Part II of this book. It requires a very successful early career, one that has left the person in a strong enough position to be able to handle the demanding leadership job. It requires a sense of one's own limitations, especially when making key strategic (diversification) decisions and implementing significant changes. And, finally, it requires sound moral judgment.

All too often, discussions of corporate social responsibility or corporate morality boil down to nothing more than an indictment against some organizations for "doing bad," with some occasional praise for a few others for "doing good." The typical conclusion drawn more and more these days by the public at large is that what we need are more top executives who will give greater priority to people and less priority to profits.[16] Period. It's simple.

Effective leadership in top posts in modern organizations demands something far more complex than the desire to "do good." It requires sound moral *judgment*. This means, first of all, a keen sense of *all* the people or groups who are affected by the firm's operations and decisions. Many will be obvious (e.g., large customers or stockholders), but some won't be (e.g., people living downstream from a plant that uses river water). It requires an appreciation of what their interests are, not just in a narrow economic sense, but in the broadest sense possible. And it requires the capacity to estimate not only the first- or even second-order consequences for all these people of decisions made by the firm, but even third, fourth, and beyond.

All the truly great business and government leaders that I have known have these capacities. And in some sense, this is what most clearly differentiates them from their talented, but more naïve or cynical colleagues.

CHAPTER 9

LATE CAREER
Letting Go Gracefully

If today's organizations are to serve us well, they require not only people who can play the kind of leadership role outlined in previous chapters, but people who are able and willing to stop playing that role at the appropriate time.

Between the ages of sixty and seventy, most people in leadership positions in modern organizations are asked to step aside—to find successors and then to pass their jobs on to these younger men and women. After wielding commendable power and being very influential for a period of ten to thirty years, many people have difficulty letting go gracefully. Some people have a great deal of difficulty. And the consequences of this problem of management succession can be very large indeed.

I

In 1946, forty-five-year-old William S. Paley became chairman and chief executive officer of CBS, Inc.[1] Over the next twenty years, he took a company with yearly revenues of less than $100 million and built it into a communications and entertainment giant with revenues of nearly a billion dollars. He also created within the broadcast group, the heart of the company, the most respected and successful television network in the world.

In 1966, when Paley reached the age of sixty-five, he did not retire. He remained in his job even though CBS had a mandatory retirement rule (which the board waived for Paley) and even though he had, in Frank Stanton, a highly respected and very well-qualified successor. Stanton was then fifty-eight and had already been president of CBS for more than two decades. Nevertheless, Paley did not step aside, nor did he even grant Stanton the title of CEO.

In 1969, John A. Schneider, a CBS veteran with over twenty years' service, was made executive vice-president. Many people believed that when Stanton reached sixty-five in 1973, the board would waive the mandatory retirement rule in his case, as it had in Paley's, make him chairman, and make Schneider president. But that didn't happen.

In 1971, Schneider left CBS. Paley has been quoted as saying that "he just did not work out. Jack's expertise and fund of knowledge was in broadcasting, and he found it difficult to cope with the intricate business and financial decisions incumbent on anyone running a complex corporation." Charles T. Ireland Jr., an acquisitions specialist working for ITT, was brought in to take Schneider's place as a successor to Stanton as president. But six months later, Ireland died of a heart attack.

In 1972, Paley formally abandoned the idea of moving aside and making Stanton chairman and CEO. "That did not work out," Paley has written. "I exercised my prerogatives to continue on in my own role. No doubt Frank was disappointed." Now, at age seventy-one, Paley moved Stanton into the post of vice-chairman in preparation for his retirement in 1973, and brought Arthur R. Taylor in from International Paper Company to be president. Taylor, who was only thirty-six years old at the time of his appointment, had been at International Paper for only two years. Before that, he had been a vice-president at First Boston Corporation for nine years.

In 1976, the broadcast group at CBS slipped into second place behind ABC in the prime-time ratings race. A young programming "genius" at ABC by the name of Fred Silverman had achieved what no one else at NBC or ABC had been able to do. Paley, now seventy-five years old, reacted very strongly. He fired Taylor and replaced him with John D. Backe, forty-six, an executive who had come to CBS in 1973 after holding top jobs at Silver Burdett Company and GE.

Between 1976 and 1979, Backe helped boost CBS revenues from $2.2 billion to $3.7 billion. He regained the prime-time ratings lead from ABC, and according to *Business Week*, began to get CBS ready for "the new era of communications that today's rapid technological developments promise in the 1980s." In the process, he impressed members of the CBS board, and won the respect of CBS affiliates. Nevertheless, late in the afternoon of May 8, 1980, seventy-eight-year-old William Paley fired Backe. Shortly thereafter, he announced that fifty-year-old Thomas Wyman, the CEO at Green Giant Co., would join CBS as president and CEO. Tom Wyman's background before Green Giant was with Polaroid. He was lured to CBS with a financial package that included a front-end bonus of $1 million and $800,000 per year in compensation guaranteed for three years.

I first met Mr. Wyman in November 1981. He had recently instituted a quarterly meeting of the fifty or so top executives at CBS—something that had never been done before. One topic for discussion at the November meeting was to be "career development." It seems that some executives in CBS were concerned that the firm was not doing a very good job of developing the next generation of managers and professionals needed to run the larger and more complex company. I was asked to speak to the group on this topic. (Mr. Paley was not at the meeting.) The top corporate human resources officer introduced me by noting that I had written an article called "Managing Your Boss," a copy of which he said he was going to give to Mr. Wyman. Everyone laughed. Very nervously.

Only after his eightieth birthday did William Paley, reluctantly and under pressure retire.

II

Perhaps an even more common example of the problem of letting go of a powerful job is the executive who "retires," but doesn't really. That is, he or she officially passes on the baton to someone else, but doesn't get out of the picture. Or he or she steps out briefly and then reappears.

A typical example would be Sidney Grossman. Mr. Grossman retired in the late 1970s as the head of a small insurance brokerage firm in Philadelphia. He turned the business over to his son and moved to Florida. Then, according to the *Wall Street Journal,* "he spent most of the next two years calling his son on the phone to complain, check up, or just to chat." [2]

Two much more visible examples of this problem are Henry Ford II and Harold Geneen. Ford had promised for years to retire on or before his sixty-fifth birthday. In a 1979 interview, he was quoted as saying that although "nobody wants to believe what I say," he was going to "hand over the reins of power at Ford" that very year, at age sixty-two.[3] He is also quoted as being firm about making a clean break. "As soon as I give up the CEO's position, I'm not going to be on any committees. I'm not going to be sitting in on policy and strategy meetings or product meetings or anything like that. I won't have anything to do with it."

To many people's surprise, Ford did actually turn the firm over to Philip Caldwell that year. And he even left his office in the automakers world headquarters (the Glass House) and moved into an office suite in Detroit's Renaissance Center, the river-front complex that he had helped develop. But he didn't disassociate himself completely. He continued on the board of directors and as chairman of the powerful finance committee. And in 1981, when Ford announced its second big annual loss in a row ($1.06 billion that year), he "quietly vacated his suite at Ren Cen" and, according to *Fortune,* moved to "one of the twin office buildings near the Glass

House, where he's close enough to do some backseat driving."

Geneen's case is more dramatic.[4] After running ITT for nearly twenty years, sixty-eight-year-old Geneen was forced by his board in 1978 to give up his job and become chairman. According to the *Wall Street Journal,* they were "concerned that Mr. Geneen's 1973 Senate testimony about the company's role with the Central Intelligence Agency in Chile could lead to a federal indictment for perjury against Mr. Geneen." For a replacement, the board chose Lyman Hamilton, the firm's chief financial officer who had been "branded Mr. Clean for his untainted career at scandal-ridden ITT." Hamilton, although somewhat surprised by this appointment, quickly got himself into the job, while a frustrated Geneen watched from the sidelines.

In March 1978, the Justice Department dropped the possibilty of prosecuting Geneen on the Chile perjury charges. "From that moment," an associate of Geneen's is quoted as saying, "Hamilton was a dead man." Indeed, within eighteen months, the ITT board asked Hamilton to step down. Apparently Geneen was disturbed at the way Hamilton was running the business and at the fact that he was not listening to Geneen's advice. So Geneen lobbied the board and, according to some people, said "It's either him or me." The board, made up mostly of people chosen by Geneen, chose Geneen.

Following Hamilton's departure, Rand V. Araskog, a forty-seven-year-old senior vice-president at ITT, was appointed president and CEO with Geneen's blessing. Within six months, Geneen retired as chairman, giving complete control officially to Araskog. But retired or not, he did not fade from the scene. He stayed on the board of directors and got a consulting contract for about $500,000 a year that ran through 1985. And, according to a *Business Week* report dated December 15, 1980, "Geneen consults often with Araskog." One former top-level director at ITT put it this way: "Some people will tell you that Geneen has no power anymore, but I say absolutely yes, he wields power."

As of this writing, seventy-two-year-old Harold Geneen, although officially retired from operating jobs, is still playing an active role at ITT.

III

It is sometimes difficult for people, especially the naïve, to understand why problems like these exist. Most of the working world looks forward to retirement. Why shouldn't these guys? Cynics think it is obvious why people don't want to let go. Who in their right mind would ever *give away* a powerful position?

A careful look at these situations suggests a number of more subtle reasons why people have difficulty letting go. First of all, when you have worked for the same firm for three, four, or even five decades, it is not uncommon to identify very strongly with the organization and to be heavily invested psychologically in it. Because of this high ego and emotional involvement, the thought of retiring can feel like abandoning one of your children, or even turning over control of a part of your body to someone else. That is, it's unthinkable.

This type of heavy ego involvement seems to be very common among entrepreneurs—people who successfully start and build firms, or who take over existing firms and literally make them into what they are today (like Geneen). It is also common in family businesses, where actually having your name on the door encourages strong identification (as in Ford's case).

Retirement is also often very difficult for people whose whole life, or whose major source of satisfaction, centers around work. Lots of successful people find that their work absorbs most of their time and energy. The very fact of their success leads them to invest more and more time and energy into work, where the payoff is high. But by doing so, they create a real problem for themselves at retirement time. With nothing to do after retirement, or with nothing to do that seems like fun, people logically look at retirement as death and resist it strongly. (This attitude is not all together irrational. Many cases have been reported over the years of very work-centered people who retired and then suddenly died shortly thereafter.)

Still another reason why some people have difficulty turning over the reins of power to others is because their finances are tied up in the business, and there is no one they trust to succeed them in managing their assets. It is not at all unusual for entrepreneurs and those running family businesses to have most of their wealth, sometimes nearly all of it, tied up in their firms. It is also not unusual for such people to be strong-willed managers who aren't very good at developing successors. So at age sixty or seventy, they find themselves fearing that retirement could, quite literally, cost them millions.

There are probably still more reasons, but the point should be clear. Powerful forces can exist to keep people from wanting to retire. And when pressure begins to develop to force them to retire, as it almost always does, these same forces sometimes lead men of integrity to take actions that can have a highly destructive impact on either their firms or specific people or both.

Nearly a decade ago, I encountered one rather tragic example of this problem. The firm involved was a moderately large service organization. It was run by a seventy-two-year-old gentleman who had been the chairman and CEO for over fifteen years. The central character in this story, however, was not this man, but the young manager of the firm's East Coast office.

This young manager had known little besides success. He had always done well in school. Since graduating from business school, he had received some type of promotion every two years. Just after his thirty-fourth birthday, he was put in charge of his company's fourth largest office. His family and friends expected him to continue to be successful. So did he.

In June of 1973, he had a meeting with his firm's chairman in which the chairman stressed the importance of not losing a particular client. At the time, the young manager thought this meeting was rather odd, since that client accounted for only one half of one percent of the firm's business. But he soon forgot about this meeting. Later, in September, he received the smallest yearly bonus he had ever received since joining the firm. At first, he thought it was obviously a mistake; in the previous year, his office had increased its sales by fifteen percent and its profits by eighteen percent at the same time that it upgraded some of its staff and added a new type of service. He subsequently found out from the firm's president that it was not a mistake—top management was "disappointed that its expressed concern for a certain client had not been satisfactorily dealt with." The client was close to dropping relations with the firm.

The young manager attempted to explain what was obvious to him: that the client was not so important to the company and that meeting management demands would cost his office much more than it would benefit the firm. The president made it very clear that he was not interested in listening to this logic. Instead, he was interested in the chairman's desire that they keep the client.

The manager immediately considered resigning. But the more he thought about it, the less attractive that alternative looked. He kept thinking of troublesome questions. How was he going to explain his resignation to others? And what would his current supervisors say when a new potential employer approached them? If the situation got ugly, what impact would that have on his career? And what impact would that have on the family that depended on him? He then began to worry that maybe the chairman had information he did not have about the importance of that one client to the firm. Was he just being stubborn, insensitive, and disloyal? What harm would it do to be sensitive to his superior's desires? Didn't he ask his employees, under some circumstances, to do things that did not make sense to them? He had his orders in this case. Why was he waiting?

In October 1974, the manager began to implement a series of decisions that shifted his and his staff's attention away from a number of clients and toward that one client. He always tried to find ways to do this so that other aspects of organizational effectiveness were not undermined. But in some cases, this was not possible. For example, he dropped three projects aimed at staff training because he was too busy. He allocated an unusually large budget for "entertainment" for the client. When one of his staff began seriously to question these moves, he had him transferred. He rationalized his actions as doing what was best for the firm. But he didn't feel good about it.

In 1975 the young manager left his firm to accept an attractive offer from a competitor. And shortly after that, he was able to find out what was really happening back at his previous employer.

It seems that his former chairman had delayed his retirement twice, at ages sixty-five and seventy. In 1973 and 1974, several members of his board of directors were putting pressure on him to retire because they felt he was no longer providing effective leadership in his job. In his efforts to cope with his dependence on the board, the chairman pointed out that the firm had held five clients successfully for over twenty years each, a very unusual situation in their industry. When he later heard that one of those five clients might soon sever relations with his firm, he set into motion the scenario affecting the young manager.

In this case, the board finally did get the chairman to step down at age seventy-five. No one really knows what other actions he took during his waning years that may have hurt the firm, its clients, or its employees. Nor do we have any way of really knowing how large the total social cost of this type of problem is. But it probably isn't small.

IV

Avoiding the kinds of problems leaders in modern organizations sometimes face in the late stages of their careers is possible. Indeed, any number of strong leaders retire successfully every year—David Rockefeller and Reg Jones (GE) are good recent examples. Some, like William S. Sneath, Harold J. Haynes, and Jack J. Crocher—the former chief executive officers at Union Carbide, Standard Oil of California, and Super Valu Stores, Inc.—even step aside long before mandatory retirement ages. When Crocher stepped down at age fifty-seven, he explained that: "I was right for the company during my time, but now I feel it needs someone more structured than I am. Mike Reed (his replacement) will be a better man for the decade ahead than I would." [5]

This kind of effective succession requires, first and foremost, considerable planning *in advance*. A flurry of activity a few months before the mandatory retirement deadline never works. Years of preparation are normally necessary to find and groom a successor, to establish appropriate postretirement activities for oneself, and to make the transition smoothly.

For example, regarding finding and grooming a successor, Edward W. Carter, the former chief executive officer at Carter Hawley Hale Stores, Inc., first met Philip M. Hawley nearly twenty years before he replaced Carter as CEO at CHH.[6] At the time, Hawley was working as a buyer for another firm. Carter hired him and, after being very impressed by his potential, transferred him among the divisions at CHH to give him experience and encouraged him to get an advanced management degree, which the company paid for. In final preparation for the succession, Carter and his board even changed the name of the firm to include "Hawley."

Successful retirement also requires carefully planning a satisfying life after leaving one's executive post. For some people, this means nothing more than a home in Arizona next to a golf course, a few friends, and an easy flight to their grandchildren. Or it means the development of hobbies that one never had time for during the earlier years (one of the activities Winston Churchill turned to was painting). But for many successful leaders, this means a whole new set of activities, outside their firms, where they can continue to exercise power and play leadership roles.

When I first met Reginald Jones, he was one year into his retirement from GE, and was as active as ever. He was a member of a dozen or so boards of directors, and participated in a wide variety of other activities. Some retired executives go into consulting. Others prefer to work outside of business. They become involved in community, civic, or philanthropic activities. For example, Wallace Rasmussen, who retired in 1979 as chief executive officer of Beatrice Foods, began serving on the board of a state prison, and has been reported to derive great satisfaction from that activity.[7]

Finally, successful retirement requires a careful transition. Indeed, the most successful retirements I have personally seen have all had the following characteristics:

1. The executives involved began turning over duties to their successors starting two to five years before their official retirement.
2. At the same time, the executives began setting up their new outside activities; they didn't wait until the last minute.
3. The transition thus occurred in a very incremental way. There were no sudden, abrupt changes that had to be adjusted to.

Probably the best way to make sure that these events occur is by having the expectation built into the very culture of the organization that they will occur. Short of that, it would benefit us all if every person in a leadership role in modern organizations stood in front of a mirror at about age fifty-five or sixty, looked himself or herself straight in the eyes, and asked if he or she were *really* preparing adequately for retirement:

- When must I, or should I, retire from my current employer for the good of the organization? How does this possibility make me feel? If the feeling is unpleasant, or if I find myself just refusing to think about it, why is that? Is it because almost all of my satisfactions in life come from this work? Or because my ego is just so wrapped up in it? Or what?
- Do I really know what kind of person the organization needs as a successor to me? Am I seriously and systematically grooming such a person, someone who can do at least as good a job as I have done? If no, why not? And what can I do to get the process started as soon as possible?
- Have I seriously thought out what kind of activities would be really satisfying for me after I retire? Have I taken any steps yet to begin to set up these activities? If not, is it because it's really too early, or am I stalling?

Obviously, for some people, facing up to this issue is a big job, one with which they often need help. In the case of chief executive officers, I personally think that the help, in the form of a certain discipline, can and should usually come from a firm's board of directors. Boards have the right and the duty to initiate and monitor the succession process. Indeed, one could argue that there are very few if any other duties that should take a higher priority. The stakes are that large.

Board involvement in management succession means, at a minimum, the following:

1. Clarifying when the CEO's retirement date will be. This can always be changed, but it should not be left vague.
2. Setting into motion some successor identification and grooming process at least three or four years before the retirement date. Ideally, this should begin seven or eight years before the retirement.
3. Monitoring that process often and in detail. This means actually meeting potential successors, signing off on plans for their development, etc.
4. At least two years before retirement, monitoring the CEO's postretirement planning.
5. Picking the successor. Allowing the CEO to do it is usually a mistake.

There are boards that take these steps, and thus accept the responsibility for providing leadership on the issue of management succession. But most boards do not. And this should change.

PART IV

IMPLICATIONS

CHAPTER 10

IMPROVING PERSONAL EFFECTIVENESS AT WORK
Some Recommendations

Implicit in the argument presented throughout this book is the belief that many of the people currently in leadership jobs, and many of those preparing themselves for such jobs, could be more effective if they thought about their work and if they managed their careers in ways that are not the norm today. In this next to the last chapter, I will summarize some of the key actions that people can take to help themselves and their employers. In the final chapter, we will look at what needs to be done by some of our major institutions to develop the quality and quantity of leadership we will need in the foreseeable future.

I

The effective management of the complex social milieu associated with professional, technical, and management jobs today demands, first and foremost, that we think about "work" in more relational terms and that we more explicitly recognize power and leadership issues.

Our ancestors were much more dependent upon nature—forces largely out of their control—than they were on other people. Their work gave them a reasonable amount of autonomy from others. Today, the opposite is true. After a century of technological, social, and economic change, we are much less dependent on nature and much more dependent on other people. Our work gives us much less autonomy. It places many of us in a web of interdependent relationships to a diverse group of others. Yet all too often, we still think of work, except that done by "managers," as a set of tasks or responsibilities that one performs pretty much by oneself. Even well-educated and fairly sophisticated observers often think of today's work organizations as being made up of a few leadership jobs which direct a cadre of management jobs which supervise masses of individual contributors (see Figure 10–1, Part A). Such misperceptions clearly impair people's effectiveness at work.

In a typical corporation today, most of the top one hundred or five hundred or, if the firm is large, one thousand jobs are complex leadership jobs. They make people dependent on a large and often diverse group of subordinates, most of whom they have little direct control over. The days when a boss said "jump," and everyone responded "how high?," are gone forever. They also make people dependent on other departments or divisions for supplies or assistance or some form of cooperation. Outside the firm, they make people dependent on important customers, key suppliers, government regulators, unions, and others—groups that often make conflicting demands. Even much lower in organizations, one typically finds many jobs that demand leadership. Positions in what is usually called middle and lower-level management make incumbents dependent on fewer people and a less diverse group of people than higher-level jobs. But they also give incumbents much less power to deal with these dependencies. So the gap is still there. And leadership is still very important. In the case of individual contributor jobs, there are few if any subordinates involved, and the job-holder usually has little if any formal power. But there are often a lot

A. THE STEREOTYPE, BASED ON HISTORICAL REALITY

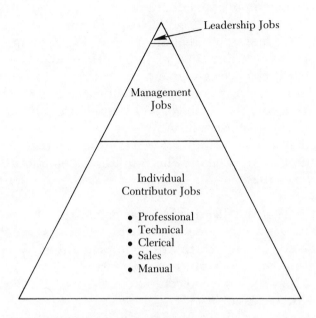

B. THE REALITY TODAY

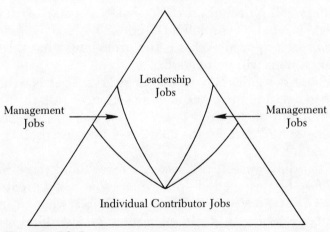

FIGURE 10–1

of lateral relationships to peers, people in other departments
or divisions, and outsiders, that are important and often pro-
blematic. And there are relationships to bosses, often many
bosses in the hierarchy, that are critical. Performing well in
these jobs requires getting all these others above one and
outside one's chain of command to do things, to cooperate,
or at least to comply. Performing well thus demands leadership even in some lower level jobs (see Figure 10–1, Part B).

Doing well in a leadership job, regardless of level or formal
title, demands an attention to relationships and to issues of
cooperation and resistance. This requires systematic attention
to issues like these:

- In terms of the decision that has been made, or the alternative we are considering, what specific tasks will need
  to be carried out for this to be implemented effectively?
  If all the necessary tasks are not entirely clear (as is often
  the case with large and complex decisions), what activities
  may be necessary?
- Whose cooperation will be needed to accomplish all these
  tasks? That is, which subordinates, peers, bosses, and outsiders will be required to do something actively if these
  tasks are to be completed effectively? Whose cooperation
  may be required? What is the probability that this additional help will be needed?
- Whose compliance will be necessary? That is, who will
  be in a position to block needed action, or stop the accomplishment of required tasks? Whose compliance *may* be
  necessary? What are the chances of needing their compliance too?
- What differences exist between myself and those people
  whose help is needed—differences that could create conflict or breed adversarial feelings? That is, what key differences exist in our goals, our values, our world views, the
  stakes we perceive we have?
- What are the underlying forces that have created these
  differences? How much is caused by differences in our
  backgrounds—social class, training, nationality, work experience, etc.? How much is caused by differences in our

jobs and in the environments in which we work—differences in the products, markets, and technologies we use, in the people with whom we interact, in the way we are evaluated and rewarded, in the goals and plans of the organizations for which we work?

- In light of the above, how likely is it that these individuals or groups will not want to do what is needed? If a problem arises, why will they resist? Are they likely to be unaware of what is needed? Do they not trust me? Are they too busy to help? Do they have conflicting stakes in the situation? (Will this decision actually hurt them? If yes, do we really want and need to do this?) Will they think this is a poor decision? If yes, why? (Is it really a good decision?)
- How strongly will they be able to resist efforts to make them cooperate? Upon what is their power in this situation based? Their jobs? Information they have? Resources they control? Their reputations or track records? Personal skills? Relationships with other people?
- Do the people who may be inclined and able to block the successful implementation of this decision have either a formal or informal relationship with me? If yes, what is the basis of my power in the relationship? Do the others feel obliged to me in certain ways? If yes, what kinds of requests on my part would they respond to favorably in light of their sense of the obligation? Do the others see me as an expert in certain areas? What areas? Do the others like me and identify with my vision of the future? If yes, how strong is this identification? Do they feel they are dependent on me in certain ways? If yes, how strong is the felt dependence and what is the basis of it?
- What other power sources do I have that can be used to help in this situation? Do I have good relationships with still other people who in turn could either help me build a stronger relationship with those people or influence them for me? If yes, which people could be most helpful in this regard? What is the nature of my relationship with each of them?
- What information do I have or can I get that may be relevant here? Do I have a clear sense of who these people

are, what differences exist between us, and where there is mutuality of interests? What tangible resources do I have that might be useful here and that others would see as legitimate to employ in this situation? What about my track record and reputation? Can I use certain aspects of them to help build a better relationship with these other people?

This kind of thinking is absolutely essential in all leadership jobs, and it is helpful in any job that contains more than a minimum level of responsibility. And this is not possible unless one thinks about work in what is often called a "big picture" way. That is, it simply is not possible to answer these questions on an ongoing basis, within a practical time limit, unless you already have most of the necessary information. And that is not likely unless one thinks about and monitors a range of people and activities far beyond one's limited job responsibilities. Indeed, the better one understands all the business issues involved, and all the people involved, the better position one is in to act responsibly and effectively.

II

In a longer-run sense, managing the social milieu at work requires competent handling of one's own career. It simply is not possible to deal effectively with the leadership challenges associated with managerial, professional, and technical careers without some advance planning.

The first step, and in some ways the most important, is to get into an industry, company, and initial career path that makes sense in light of your own background, interests, temperament, and skills. To take an extreme example, if the ideas in Chapter 6 on managing bosses make you want to throw up, then you had better try to get into a career situation that allows for considerable independence from bosses (my own job is a good example). To do otherwise is surely not in anyone's best interests.

Getting into an occupational environment that fits one's strengths, weaknesses, values, and needs demands self-assessment and opportunity assessment. This means thinking hard about issues such as:

- How much experience have I had so far in dealing with peer, boss, subordinate, and other work relationships? More specifically, what is the largest number of bosses I've ever had at one time? The largest number of peer or lateral relationships? The largest number of subordinates?
- How successfully have I dealt with these dependent relationships? Specifically, how many and what kinds of problems have I had with bosses? Subordinates? Peers and others? For example, have I had a history of difficulty with bosses in general? If yes, how do the problems typically manifest themselves? How does my behavior contribute to the difficulty? Have I had problems with peers under any circumstance? If yes, is there a pattern that relates to either the characteristics of the other people (i.e., age, sex, national origin, experience level, etc.) or with characteristics of the situation (i.e., how closely you had to work with them, the time pressures involved, etc.)?
- Have problems areas tended to go away over time as I got more experience and, hence, are probably caused by lack of awareness and/or skill? Or have certain kinds of problems persisted despite more experience and, hence, are probably related to something deeper and less likely to change?
- In terms of the employment options that are possible, how does each organization rate on those dimensions that create diversity, interdependence, conflict, power struggles, and political processes? How many different products, services, markets, and technologies are involved? How complex are the technologies? How much is each organization at the mercy of bankers, government and union officials, competitors, and large customers? How large and diverse are the labor forces involved? How much job specialization is there in each case? How many levels are there in the management hierarchy?
- What would be the exact nature of the relationship de-

mands in the specific entry-level jobs that are possible?
For each job, how many bosses would be relevant? Peers
and outsiders? Subordinates? How dependent would I be
made on these people? How diverse a group are they?
How different are they from me?

Once into an appropriate situation, sensible career management means always thinking ahead a few steps, then planning for these moves (right up to and through retirement),
and getting the appropriate people committed to your plans
(especially bosses). It also means, each time you take a step
and are new on a job, even greater than usual attention to
developing relationships with all the appropriate people involved and not falling into the trap of tackling some problem
before you have the clout to be able to solve it.

And before making each job shift, effective career management means very carefully evaluating the appropriateness of
the change. It is essential not to be seduced into a job for
which you are not prepared. And that demands that even
before seeking (much less accepting) a new job assignment,
one consider the following:

- Given the responsibilities inherent in the job and relevant
  goals for the position in the immediate future, upon whom
  would the job make me dependent and to what degree?
  What bosses would be important? Which peers and outsiders? How many subordinates?
- How big are the differences between myself and the person who will be my boss? (Is it possible that they are
  hopelessly large?) Is the boss at least as competent and
  powerful as his or her peers? (If not, what kinds of problems could this create for me?) If there is more than one
  relevant boss involved, how well do they agree on goals
  and policies? How well do they get along? Are there any
  really strong animosities?
- What power comes with the job? That is, what kind of
  a budget is guaranteed? What authority over which decisions is guaranteed?
- What is required to perform at an excellent level in the

new job? Specifically, what information is needed? What
relationships are essential? What skills are key?
- What relevant power sources do I bring to the job? How
much do I really know about the products, services, markets, people, and technologies associated with the job's
responsibilities? How good are my relationships with all
of the people upon whom the job would make me dependent? How relevant is my track record? My reputation?
My personal skills?
- How many more relevant assets can be realistically developed during the first six to eight months on the job? Will
all this be enough, or am I potentially putting myself in
a position where I cannot make up the power gap, where
I cannot provide effective leadership, and thus where I
simply cannot do the job adequately, with all the associated consequences for myself, the firm, and my family?

This kind of thinking, which explicitly takes into account
important power and influence issues, is especially essential
if one is going to establish and maintain the kind of success
syndrome needed to play an important leadership role in organizations. Although I'm sure some very successful executives
would vigorously deny ever thinking this way (because it is
not fashionable or wise to appear to be too concerned with
power issues), a careful examination of their career moves
will usually show a pattern that is entirely consistent with
this line of analysis.

III
Finally, and perhaps most importantly, effective and responsible handling of today's complex jobs demands a realistic
appreciation of why so many people have so many power-
related problems at work. The reason, which is not fully understood by the naïve or the cynical, is directly related to how
much the very nature of work has changed in the past century
due to the emergence of the modern organization.

Of course, organizations of some size and complexity have
existed for at least six thousand of the million or so years that
humans have lived on earth. Egyptian governments that built

pyramids and the Catholic Church are perhaps the best-known examples of this. But until the last hundred years or so, the number of these organizations, their size and complexity, and the percentage of the population working within them, has remained very small.

As recently as 1820 in the United States, very few organizations of any size and complexity existed. There were, of course, federal and state governments, but they were relatively small. There were some factories, mostly mills, but there were not many of them, and they were relatively simple organizations compared to the plants one finds today. Overall, well under ten percent of the labor force worked in organizations employing ten or more people. The vast majority of the work force—farmers—were self-employed.

Looking at the conditions that existed then, it is easy to see why so few organizations of any size and complexity existed.[1] First of all, markets were severely limited. There weren't that many people around; the entire population of the United States in 1820 was 9,638,453. The population density was low (Washington, D.C. had a population of only 13,247) and good transportation and communication facilities didn't exist; it took over a month to get from New Orleans to Washington. Most people didn't have much money to spend on goods and services; most people were poor farmers. And big industrial markets didn't yet exist; there were no big corporations.

Furthermore, the methods, machines, tools, and power sources needed to produce a large volume of goods and services more efficiently than a small volume generally did not exist, or were uneconomical. The only economical source of power for a factory was still water from rivers. Even in 1840, the cost per horsepower for the power produced by steam engines was five to six times greater than that for the power provided by water. Computers were more than a century away in 1820, and even less sophisticated methods of processing the kinds of information required to manage a complex organization did not exist. Sources of capital for a producer of goods or services interested in expanding were limited, and methods for organizing and managing even moderate-sized enterprises were still unknown. Because of these and other reasons, it is hardly surprising that complex organizations did not exist in any number.

These conditions found in 1820 began to change rapidly in the decades before the Civil War. First, there was a great deal of technological change. During the 1850s, for example, more than twenty-five hundred patents were issued each year in the United States compared to an average of only seventy-seven during the first two decades of the existence of the Patent Office. These inventions included such varied things as the sewing machine (1846), the vulcanization of rubber (1839), and a method for canning evaporated milk (1853). But perhaps the single most important development during this period was the emergence of the railroad and telegraph. By 1860, thirty thousand miles of railroad track had been laid, most of it during the previous ten years. Almost overnight, goods, passengers, and mail could move over land much faster and more reliably than ever before. And because of the telegraph, people could, for the first time, communicate almost instantaneously over long distances. To supervise the multiple operating units associated with these businesses and to moderate the flow of people, goods, and information, new administrative structures and business procedures were developed. Also, the railroads' unprecedented capital requirements led to the emergence and growth of the first modern capital markets in the United States. During the same period, the population and the population density also grew very rapidly. Famine in Ireland and unrest in Germany sent millions of people to America. Altogether, between 1820 and 1860, the population increased by over 300 percent to 31.5 million.

All of these changes helped encourage even more change. The vastly improved communication and transportation systems, the new technologies, the new organization forms, and the larger population set off what historian Alfred Chandler has called "a revolution in production and distribution." [2] In the 1860s large department stores, such as Macy's in New York, Filene's in Boston, and Marshall Field's in Chicago, began to appear. In the 1870s, Andrew Carnegie built steel works. In the 1880s, meat producers such as Armour and Swift created national marketing networks.

Economic growth, technological developments, and population growth continued to fuel this overall process right into this century. Manufacturing, transportation, distribution, and communications organizations continued both to multiply and to grow. And in the process of growth, the typical organization evolved in the following ways: [3] First it incorporated more and more diverse activities. That is, it added more products or services for more different markets using more different technologies. Organizationally, it became more specialized, more formalized, and more decentralized. That is, it added more and more specialized jobs as it became possible to afford full-time specialists in different areas. It added more and more rules and procedures to help control the larger and more complex organization. And it pushed authority down the ever taller hierarchy as it became less and less possible for a few top officials to make all the decisions in a sensible way.

In addition, during this century and especially since World War II, more and more organizations have emerged that either provide services for the growing population of large corporations or were established to control them. Among the former are CPA firms, consulting firms, advertising agencies, and investment banks. Among the latter are local, state, and federal governmental units. And most of these organizations, unlike their predecessors, have employed a large percentage of their labor forces in professional, technical, and managerial jobs.

In total, these developments over the past century and a half have left us with a world dominated by complex organizations, organizations that now employ well over ninety percent of the labor force in the United States. And the typical organization today, from the small retail establishment employing only thirty people to the gigantic multinational manufacturing firm employing many thousands of people, is getting more complex and more dominant all the time.

These changes were not anticipated by most people then and are not really appreciated by most people now.

The very idea of a single firm employing a hundred thousand people in thousands of different kinds of jobs located all over the world, directed by thousands of managers, serving millions of customers, owned by hundreds of thousands of individuals would have seemed absurd to most people two centuries ago and would have simply been incomprehensible to others a thousand years ago. The concept of thousands of accountants all working for the same professional accounting firm would have seemed equally silly to accountants themselves only a century ago. Indeed, some people as late as World War II would have been shocked by a description of today's Big Eight accounting firms. Even the idea of some very small modern organizations—a new high-technology firm, for example, which employs less than fifty people, half of whom have twenty to twenty-one years of formal education, and which is building a new type of microcomputer—would have been completely alien before the time of our grandparents or great-grandparents.

Of course, most of us recognize without effort that some things have obviously changed since the days of our great-grandparents. We know that they did not drive automobiles or fly in airplanes or watch television. Life was more complex physically and more difficult economically for most of them. But when it comes to less visible and tangible changes, our minds tend to blur. In particular, we do not generally appreciate how radically different from today's was the social milieu in which they worked.

We often forget that, until a century ago, people generally worked by themselves and for themselves. As farmers (most of them were farmers), shopkeepers, merchants, or professionals, almost all worked in "organizations" with less than a dozen people, were given considerable autonomy, and interacted with relatively few people on a regular basis. Because of the simple technologies employed and the relative homogeneity of the people involved, their interactions tended to be rather uncomplicated. Indeed, the majority of the work force (farmers) typically spent most of their time working alone, and typically interacted with only a few people on a regular basis as a part of their work. Those other people were often much like themselves in terms of educational background and social class. And because of the small number of products, markets, and technologies involved, interactions were rather straight-forward.

Contrasting this situation with the social milieu of the work-place for an increasingly large number of people today, one finds gigantic differences. As we have seen throughout this book, many jobs in modern organizations allow little auton-omy. They require that people spend most of their time inter-acting with other people. Sometimes this means hundreds or even thousands of people. These people may be a highly heterogeneous group in terms of training, orientation, and social background. And the nature of the communication and interaction, because of all the different technologies, products, markets, and people involved, can be incredibly complex. The leadership challenge in millions of jobs is a big one.

It is useful to remind ourselves periodically of these facts because of their terribly important implications when they are considered along with other key historical realities. Our cultural (religious and moral) roots go back thousands of years, long before complex organizations dominated people's lives. Our biological roots go back millions of years. As a result, not a small number of the forces which influence our beliefs and our behavior today were formed in environments that were in some ways radically different from the environment many of us work in today. These forces make people feel uncomfortable in modern organizations. They make us yearn for the "good old days" when interpersonal lives at work were much simpler, when people had more autonomy, when one didn't have to deal with those "narrow-minded" people in accounting, those "sleazy backslapping" salesmen, the "damn" union, the "bureaucrats" in Washington, the "unfair" Japanese competitors, the "idiots" in the front office, and so on. These forces lead us to dream about dropping out, finding a simpler life, moving to a cabin in the mountains or onto a small farm.

These forces are especially powerful in the United States where the geography and history have created a culture which still idolizes the strong, silent, and independent cowboy or rancher. This stands in sharp contrast to Japan, for example, where a small, isolated, and resource-poor geography forced more interdependence among people and created a very different culture.[4]

An appreciation of these forces and the historical reasons for them can surely help us to be more patient with ourselves and others as we attempt to put into practice the recommendations made in this chapter. It can surely help us to put into a more realistic perspective our successes and failures. It can surely help us to react, at least to some degree, less naïvely and less cynically.

CHAPTER 11

LEADERSHIP AS
SOCIAL CAPITAL
An Agenda for the Future

CIVILIZATION as we know it has always needed people who could play effective and responsible leadership roles. But today this need is greater than ever. Two centuries ago, only a few hundred people would have been required to fill all the really important leadership positions on earth. Today, with a world population of over four billion, and with complex organizations dominating the scene, we need hundreds of thousands, possibly even millions of people to fill all the major leadership positions. Today, leadership is a centrally important social resource.

Many individuals can become better leaders by thinking about leadership in complex organizations in the terms used in this book, and by attending to the issues raised in the previous chapters. But more than self-directed individual reflection and development is needed. We must also work toward creating the conditions under which this critical social resource can grow and thrive.

184

I

The development of leadership potential begins at birth. Attitudes and skills learned during the first five to ten years can make it easy or virtually impossible for an individual to play an important leadership role in adulthood. The responsibility here lies largely with us as parents. It is a most complex and challenging responsibility.

During their first few years of life, children are incredibly dependent on those around them. They have great needs that they cannot possibly meet by themselves. Quite literally, the stakes involve life or death. But because their needs are so demanding, not even the most responsive parent, grandparent, or sibling can satisfy them all the time. So sometimes they are inadvertently hurt by these people. And sometimes they are purposely punished by others in an attempt to teach habits necessary for survival. As a result, virtually all people are hurt many times at a very impressionable age by the powerful figures in their lives. And some people, because their families are unusually unresponsive either due to economic or psychological reasons, get hurt very deeply.

Psychologists have long ago established that injury early in life by powerful others can lead to strong ambivalent feelings about power, powerful people, and power and influence processes. These feelings in turn can become intellectualized as beliefs that "power always corrupts," that "the powerful cannot be trusted," and that "people who seek power do so only to exploit others." Or they can get intellectualized in almost the opposite way. In such cases people believe there is only so much power in the world, that those who don't have it are entirely vulnerable, and hence that all life is a zero-sum competition with others for power.

These cynical beliefs lead people either to seek complete dominance over others or complete autonomy from others, neither of which is feasible in modern organizations. So inevitably this leads to misdirected energy and frustration. When such people are in positions of influence over younger people, these beliefs can also lead to dysfunctional lessons being passed on to the next generation.

We would all benefit if more parents more consistently kept the following in mind:

- First of all, that children's temperamental feelings about "bosses" are strongly, probably permanently, shaped by parent-child interactions. You can raise the most intelligent, the most morally upright, the most charitable child possible, and yet still not raise a person who can play a useful leadership role in complex organizations, if the child comes to see bosses as enemies to be fought or god-like creatures to be obeyed at any cost.
- With nuclear families becoming smaller and smaller in the developed countries, more and more children will spend their early years in environments in which there are no peers or, in the form of significantly younger brothers and sisters, "subordinates." This shifts the burden to parents to find favorable settings in which their children can learn to deal effectively with peers, and in which they can begin to experience the responsibilities of leading others younger than they. I say "favorable" settings, because just throwing children into a crowd of other youngsters certainly does not guarantee that they will learn the correct lessons.
- Naïveté and cynicism rub off quickly and easily on children, unless one works carefully to contain and control those attitudes. If all a child learns about "work" comes from a parent's rantings and ravings born of frustration after a difficult day on the job, the child is bound to develop cynical attitudes. Likewise, if children hear nothing about their parents' jobs, or if they are given only simplistic answers to their inquiries about "what mommy and daddy do at work," they are going to be programmed with naive beliefs.
- Between the ages of five and twenty-one, children spend more time with educators than they do with their parents. Hence, it is an essential responsibility of parents to make sure that those educators are doing their jobs well. All too often parents behave like sheep in front of educational "experts." Such a stance serves no one well.

II

Because of their frequent contact with children, educators bear a large responsibility for the development of leadership capital. Some individual teachers, some elementary and secondary school systems, and some universities seem to do an admirable job in this regard. But that is not the norm.

Think for a moment about how educational organizations typically operate. A student's "job" involves attending classes, obeying certain simple rules while in class, doing homework, and passing objective tests. In this role, students are made dependent upon instructors, but this dependence is minimized and downplayed in most cases by the stress placed on objectivity and clarity. As long as they come to class, do not disrupt others, and answer unambiguous questions on tests (using information that they can usually learn from books independent of the instructor), they are told they are doing their jobs well. Dependence on fellow students is generally minimized. Although in most cases there are some group tasks, and some people become involved in group sports, that is not the norm, and the performance evaluation system (tests) typically ignores these activities. Furthermore, almost no one is required to lead or direct others. And for the few who do, as class officers or team captains, again the performance evaluation system basically ignores this aspect of their activity.

Of course, all of this work is done inside what are often large and complex organizations that include many other people—support staff, administrative officials, and the like. But generally, students are shielded from these people and their activities. They do not have to deal with them. For the most part, the support staff and the issues with which they deal are simply not visible to students.

These educational experiences program certain lessons about work in organizations into most people, lessons that are largely consistent with our cultural and biological roots and largely inconsistent with the reality in modern organizations for a growing number of people. The message delivered by educational organizations can be summarized, roughly, as follows: First of all, "work" means performing some task or tasks largely by oneself, even though the work is often done with other people present. Because all the needed tools are supplied, because the goals and rules are clearly specified, and because performance appraisal is "objective," securing cooperation from others is not an important issue. Neither is paying close attention to people or relationships. Granted, one shouldn't ignore people, because interacting (at least with some of them) can be rewarding. But that does not have anything to do with work. Under these conditions, leadership is not important. Complex power and influence processes have no legitimate place.

What is particularly remarkable about this absolutely dysfunctional programming is that it is provided by almost all educational organizations, even the very best! I recently brought up this subject while talking to some friends who live in an affluent Boston suburb. They have one child who is in the fourth grade in a school system that is excellent by international standards. His school provides a report card to parents four times a year. The card has about fifty items on it. Approximately forty of these grade how well the student is doing in a particular subject area (e.g., mathematics, reading, science, art, etc.). Of the remainder, most deal with how well the child takes orders from the teacher. One says something about how well the child "gets along" with peers. No item deals directly with any of the issues and skills discussed in Part II of this book. Not one!

High schools and universities are generally no better in this regard. They sanction "extracurricular activities" in which people can learn something about leadership. But they tend not to supervise these activities, and even when they do, they don't give students feedback on their leadership behavior.

We expect a lot from educators, and I'm sure some people would say that it simply is not fair or realistic to add more responsibilities. But given the amount of time children spend during their most formative years in educational institutions, we must demand that those institutions help cultivate and develop leadership skills. If this seems like an overwhelming task to educators, then we must do a better job of selecting, training, and compensating, teachers so that they can handle this responsibility.

III

Unlike other educators, management educators in our universities explicitly accept the responsibility for helping to develop leadership potential. They do so through courses on interpersonal behavior and group dynamics and by means of concepts like "communication," "participation," and "motivation." All too often, unfortunately, their material is naïve.

Both interpersonal behavior and group dynamics, as they are written about and taught in management education, tend to deal with face-to-face relations among a small number of people in relatively simple settings. Rarely are they discussed in contexts that are comparable to modern organizations, contexts that include large numbers of people, complex and sometimes ambiguous tasks, a high degree of job specialization, great interdependence among individuals who sometimes are physically thousands of miles apart, sophisticated information and machine technologies, as well as formal structures and systems and procedures.

Concepts like communication, participation, and motivation can certainly be useful, but they tend not to direct attention to some critically important questions and problems unless they are explicitly considered as aspects of power, influence, and leadership strategies. For example, the concept of communication by itself focuses attention on questions of how to increase the volume and clarity of information going from one person (or group) to another. It does not tend to direct attention to questions such as: Why do effective leaders sometimes deliberately communicate in ambiguous ways? Why is no communication at all sometimes a very powerful way to influence events? When used outside of a power and influence context, participation, like communication, also has a "more is obviously better" quality to it. By itself, this concept rarely leads to an exploration of the incredibly subtle choices that leaders face regarding involving others in their activities. The critical questions of who should (or should not) be involved, in what way, at what time, for what purpose, are rarely explored in any depth. Motivation not only shares this "more is better" quality, but like participation, it tends to direct attention downward. The question addressed is almost always,

"How does a boss motivate subordinates?" Motivation, participation, and still other popular concepts do not tend to focus attention on key issues such as: How do effective managers and professionals successfully influence their bosses to give them the information, resources, and support they need?

To some degree, the problem here is related to the naïveté and cynicism engendered by early experiences at home and in school. Lack of realistic leterature or training reinforces the naïveté and cynicism, which in turn restricts thinking, research, and writing on relevant topics, since the naïve usually do not think such topics are necessary or important, and the cynical often think it is in their best interests not to let others learn about such things. It is a selfperpetuating cycle out of which we must break.

IV

After college or graduate school, the burden for creating environments conducive to leadership development shifts to employers. Although small organizations typically do very little to nurture and develop leaders, all large corporations take some steps in this regard. But not one of the firms with which I am familiar does an adequate job. Not one!

Developing sufficient competent leadership to run a corporation requires many things, most of which are well known. It demands hiring managerial, professional, and technical people who have the potential to do more than just entry-level jobs. It requires helping those people get on board, learn the ropes, and develop an appreciation for the nature of the complex social milieu around them. It means aiding individuals in the development of power bases and a success syndromes. It requires making sure they do not get in over their heads, or stagnate in their positions.

To some degree, a strong and competent human resource group can be extremely helpful in this regard. Because members of a human resource group do not operate under the same short-run financial pressures that plague line managers, they can more easily keep their attention focused on this broader and longer-term objective. They can design and help run hiring, orientation, training, and career management programs that are structured to develop future leaders. Most large firms do all this to some degree. But few do an adequate job.

All too often recruiting and selection programs aim at getting "good" people, with no clear idea of what *good* means or should mean in the context of future corporate needs. Orientation and training programs too often serve up naïve offerings, which are more harmful than beneficial. The disparity between what people are often told in these programs and the reality in which they work predictably makes them cynical about education and training. Career management and "high potential" programs are often programs on paper only; they have very little impact on what goes on in organizations.

The problem here in many cases is that to make these programs work, the human resource staff must have a sufficient number of competent leaders in it. We must face up to the fact that naïve "social workers," "professionals" whose role-model is the powerful and autocratic M.D., and failures from other departments who have been dumped into personnel, cannot do the job.

But even with a well-functioning human resources staff, the bulk of the responsibility has to fall on the line. Line managers are in the best position to be mentors, sponsors, coaches, and role-models. Some play this role exceptionally well. But if we are to produce more people capable of dealing effectively with power gaps, we must systematically increase the amount of competent mentoring that goes on. It seems to me that it would help if all executives would periodically consider these questions:

- How many of the senior people in our firm really do an excellent job of mentoring, coaching, role-modeling, etc.? How many are really good at helping young people develop and maintain success syndromes? How many do an excellent job of teaching young people with high potential what they should and should not be focusing on early in their careers? How many of our senior people really take the time to help junior people learn about the business, make useful contacts, and develop important management skills?

- Given the number of people we will need in leadership roles in ten or twenty years, is enough good mentoring going on now? Are enough junior people getting the attention they need? If not, why not? And what practical steps can we take to improve the situation?

I'm willing to bet that most firms would find the answers to these questions quite sobering.

Of course, the very best of mentoring will not make up for strategic and structural decisions that create unmanageable amounts of diversity and interdependence, a large number of huge power gaps, and the like. So the final requirement for developing the leadership we need in the future is that we not make the leadership task an impossible one. This means we have got to stop thinking about corporations as "portfolios" of business that can be managed effectively by financial geniuses. And we must stop viewing government bureaucracies as only "instruments" for implementing the brilliant programs designed by elected officials and their staffs. Both private and public organizations are complex human systems that can be made unmanageable. We must not allow this to happen.

ACKNOWLEDGMENTS
(With a Brief Description of the
History of the Book)

THIS book has roots in seven different research and course development projects conducted during the 1970s and 1980s at Harvard Business School. These projects involved dozens of individuals, many of whom have made important contributions to this book.

The very first inquiry, launched in 1971 and completed in 1974, focused on mayors in twenty large U.S. cities.[1] This was historical research, since we chose not to study people currently in office, but rather individuals who had served during the 1960s. The cities involved included Atlanta, Buffalo, Cincinnati, Cleveland, Columbus, Dallas, Fort Worth, Houston, Indianapolis, Jersey City, Kansas City, Louisville, Minneapolis, New Haven, New Orleans, Newark, Norfolk, Rochester, San Diego, and San Franscisco. By interviewing people who were close to the action—newspaper reporters, city officials, business and labor leaders, and many others—Paul Lawrence and I tried to identify the challenges modern mayors faced, how these elected officials approached their work, and what impact they had on their communities. It was a stimulating study for us, at least partially because almost all of our prior experience had been in the private sector. To some degree this project reinforced and extended previous work by Lawrence,[2] especially regarding the question of how situationally specific effective ways of organizing are. But in addition, the project helped launch a new line of inquiry, one that focused on power, influence, and leadership in complex settings.

It is almost incredible how complex these mayoral jobs were. Limited resources, conflicting demands from various constituencies, an unending number of distractive power struggles, and many other factors made achieving anything difficult. Yet in a few cases—not many—the mayors were able to orchestrate achievements of which both they and the residents of their cities were very proud. To understand all this, we found that one needed above all to appreciate the issue of power—its development and its use. Put succinctly, the more effective mayors were more successful in developing and using power to lead a large and complex network of people and groups. In contradiction to the popular stereotype, the strong mayors were not the ones who became involved in scandals, graft, and corruption; it was the weak mayors who were vulnerable and often desperate.

In 1974, a project was designed to follow up the mayors study. A group of twenty-six organizations ultimately participated in this inquiry, organizations of various sizes and ages in retailing, banking, consulting, advertising, electronics manufacturing, health care, education, heavy-equipment manufacturing, insurance, communications, food, clothing, the arts, government, power generation, investment management, and consumer products manufacturing. In each case, the top ten to twelve officials were interviewed and as much documentation on the organization as practical was obtained. Ultimately, this information was analyzed from two perspectives. The first focused on questions of how these organizations evolved, developed, and changed over time.[3] The second dealt explicitly with issues relating to the acquisition and use of power by managers.[4] By the time the project was completed, any doubt in my mind was gone about the relevance to the private and nonprofit sectors of much I had seen in the public sector.

The public-private distinction is both useful and distracting. It is useful in that, at the extremes, what one finds in the public sector—no bottom line profitability standard, for example—can be very different from what one finds in the private sector. It is distracting because it downplays similarities, and there can be many similarities. Although the problems caused by conflicting demands, resource constraints, and power struggles are usually more severe in the public sector, they also clearly exist in private and nonprofit organizations. Furthermore, I found that the general "solution" to coping with such problems was the same, too. Wanting very much to make a difference, although a necessary condition, was far from sufficient. Both studies suggested that one also needed a strong sensitivity to the complex social milieu in which one operated, as well as skill at the development and use of power and influence.

During 1975, while still working on the twenty-six-organizations study, I took over our required MBA course entitled Organizational Problems. At the time, this course was not viewed very favorably by either students or faculty. Jay Lorsch, then the head of the Organizational Behavior area at Harvard, encouraged us to try something new. Over the next three years, a group of people, including Len Schlesinger, Vijay Sathe, Mike Beer, Roosevelt Thomas, and Victor Faux, began a case development effort in a number of well-known U.S. companies. Previous work by Lorsch (and Lawrence) helped guide the course development effort in at least one very important way. It sensitized us to two important dimensions that create complexity in the social milieu associated with modern organizations: (1) diversity (of beliefs, goals, values, skills, etc., among the people involved) and (2) interdependence (among those people). By focusing more on those dimensions, and by including more issues explicitly associated with power, influence, and leadership, the managerial behavior we were documenting became more understandable. Actions that were difficult to explain or interpret, especially those connected with organizational change efforts, began to fall into patterns.[5]

Running in parallel with these first three projects was another line of inquiry which did not focus on questions of power, influence, and leadership, but instead on the topic of career development in managerial and professional jobs. This career development work began for me in 1969, under the supervision of Ed Schein at MIT.[6] My first major project, however, was launched in 1972 at Harvard under the direction of Tony Athos. He, Charles McArthur, and I set about to develop materials for a new MBA elective which we subsequently called Self-Assessment and Career Development. This course development work went on for three or four years, involved Victor Faux, Warren Wilhelm, and others, and eventually produced dozens of documented cases relating to the career development of managers and professionals.[7] In 1973, in conjunction with this work, a longitudinal research project was started, the subjects of which were 130 members of the Harvard MBA class of 1974. This study, which continues today in collaboration with Jeff Sonnenfeld, has relied primarily on detailed yearly questionnaires, supplemented by interviews and standard psychological instruments, to learn about these people and the development of their lives over time.[8]

Two themes emerged early in this work. The first relates to "job/person fit." Whenever the people we studied moved into situations that did not fit their skills, interests, expectations, needs, and experiences to some minimum degree, problems arose, regardless of how talented the individuals were in a general sense, and regardless of how much they really wanted to succeed, be effective, or make a difference. The second theme relates to "career stages"—to the fact that some of the issues, problems, and challenges people face in their work lives tend to be predictably different at different stages in their careers, and that a sensitivity to these stage-specific issues can help one deal with those issues more effectively.

It was not until the late 1970s that these two streams of research—one on career development, the other on leadership and power—clearly began to merge. This first occurred in what was called the General Managers' Research Project.

Started in 1976, this five-year study looked in some depth at fifteen successful general managers in nine different companies.[9] These fifteen executives ranged in age from thirty-seven to sixty-two and, on average, were paid a yearly salary of $150,000 in 1978 dollars. Unlike previous work, this project used, in addition to interviews, questionnaires, and documents, a considerable amount of observation. That is, each of these executives was actually observed in action over a period of time.

Themes associated with the complexity of the social milieu inside modern organizations, with power and the importance of influence skills, and with job-person fit, were all confirmed and extended in this study. Furthermore, the project clearly showed us that to understand why these successful managers were able to behave as they did, it was essential to understand their career and early-life histories. That is, to account for similarities and differences in their leadership styles, their use of power, and their ability to influence others, one had to look at similarities and differences in their career and childhood development.

The seventh and final project upon which this book is built was begun in 1978. Based on the previous work, I decided to develop a new MBA course called Power and Influence. Over the following four years, a few dozen new field-based cases were developed, many with assistance from John Stengrevics; and this book was begun.

Of the additional insights developed in this final project, four are particularly important. First of all, in thinking about managing the social milieu surrounding a job, I found it is useful to distinguish relationships with bosses from those with peers or outsiders from those with subordinates.[10] The issues involved in each case vary, as does the appropriate way of dealing with them. The second insight relates to the central task in the initial career stage, that period most people experience between the ages of twenty and forty. For people who aspire to make a real difference in professional and managerial jobs in complex organizations, the central issue during this period seems to be developing an adequate power base. The third insight came from actually teaching the material contained in this book to MBAs and to practicing managers. Over time, it became clearer and clearer that a large percentage of these people were surprisingly naïve about this subject matter. A smaller group embraced equally inaccurate cynical beliefs. In both cases, the distorting lenses they wore created problems both for them and for those with whom they interacted. The fourth and final insight was inspired by my rereading some of Al Chandler's work on the historical evolution of modern management and the modern business organization. This led to an examination of how managerial, professional, and technical jobs have been changing with respect to issues of power and leadership over the last century, and especially in the last three or four decades. This exploration eventually led to the central thesis of the book.

Overall, therefore, this book has a history that spans over a dozen years. It is built upon a number of R&D projects generously supported by the Harvard Business School, and its leadership—most notably including Larry Fouraker, John McArthur, Richard Walton, Richard Rosenbloom, Ray Corey, Jay Lorsch, and Paul Lawrence. It has benefited enormously from the observations and ideas of hundreds of managers and students of management, as well as from the previous work of a number of social scientists (and applied social scientists). Chief among the latter are Edward Banfield, Peter Blau, Robert Dahl, Richard Emerson, James March, David McClelland, Henry Mintzberg, Richard Neustadt, Jeff Pfeffer, Leonard Sayles, Ed Schein, Rosemary Stewart, and Karl Weick.[11] And early drafts of this book have been significantly improved through the helpful comments of Tony Athos, Tom Bonoma, Richard Boyatzis, Alan Frohman, Jack Gabarro, Vijay Sathe, Len Schlesinger, and Jeff Sonnenfeld.

NOTES

Chapter 2

1. This and other quotes and allegations about Johns-Manville are from "Shootout at the Johns-Manville Corral" by Herbert E. Meyer, *Fortune*, October 1976.
2. This material about Jones, Day is taken from "The Split: A True Story of Washington Lawyers" by Nicholas Lemann, *Washington Post Magazine*, March 23, 1980.
3. The report is based on "ABC Covers Itself," by Roy Rowan, *Fortune*, November 17, 1980.
4. See, for example, Melville Dalton, *Men Who Manage*, John Wiley, 1959, and Andrew Pettigrew, *The Politics of Organizational Decision Making*, Tavistock, 1973.
5. The central importance of the two concepts "diversity" and "interdependence" was originally brought to my attention through the work of Jay Lorsch. See *Managing Diversity and Interdependence* by Lorsch and Steven A. Allen, Harvard Business School, 1973.

6. See, for example, "The Changing Role of the Chief Executive" by A. Brearley, *Journal of General Management,* 1976, 3 (4), pp. 62–71.
7. See "ATT Marketing Men Find Their Star Fails to Ascend as Expected" by Monica Langley, *Wall Street Journal,* February 13, 1984, p. 1.

Chapter 3

1. Jeffrey Pfeffer and Robert Miles, among others, have made similar arguments. See Pfeffer's *Power in Organizations,* Pitman, 1981, and Miles's *Macro-Organizational Behavior,* Goodyear, 1980.
2. In a poll of CEOs taken in 1981, *Fortune* ranked GE and IBM as the two best-run corporations in America. See "CEOs Pick the Best CEOs," by Ann Morrison, *Fortune,* May 4, 1981, pp. 133–135.
3. See *The Gamesman,* by Michael Maccoby, Simon & Schuster, New York, 1976.
4. The useful concept of "Stakeholder" was brought to my attention by Paul Lawrence, Mike Beer, Quinn Mills, and Dick Walton, all of whom have helped develop our Human Resource Management course here at Harvard.

Chapter 4

1. This aspect of leadership and management in modern organizations has traditionally been almost ignored by those writing on these subjects. (See *Leadership: Where Else Can We Go?* edited by Morgan W. McCall Jr. and Michael Lombardo, Duke University Press, 1978.) Yet, the evidence is clear that lateral relations to peers (see *Managerial Behavior* by Leonard Sayles, McGraw-Hill, 1964) and to outsiders (see "Managing External Dependence" by John Kotter, *Academy of Management Review,* 1979, Vol. 4, No. 1, pp. 87–92) are very important and pervasive.
2. See "Choosing Strategies for Change" by John P. Kotter and Leonard A. Schlesinger, *Harvard Business Review,* July/August 1979.
3. The description is taken from case 9–1, in *Organization* by John Kotter, Leonard Schlesinger, and Vijay Sathe, Irwin, 1979.

4. See *Decision Making at the Top* by Gordon Donaldson and Jay Lorsch, Basic Books, 1983.
5. See *Power In Management* by Kotter.
6. The description is taken from Case 3–2, Alcon Laboratories, in *Organization* by John Kotter, Leonard Schlesinger, and Vijay Sathe, Irwin, 1979.
7. "The World of David Rockefeller," on "Bill Moyers' Journal," PBS, produced by David Grubin.
8. For a more detailed description of such jobs, see "Fred Fischer" by John Stengrevics and John Kotter, HBS Case Services #9–480–045.
9. The facts in this case are taken from "The Unlikely Hero of McGraw-Hill" by Donald D. Holt, *Fortune,* May 21, 1979, pp. 97–108.

Chapter 5

1. See, for example, *Stogdill's Handbook of Leadership,* 2nd edition by Bernard Bass, Free Press, 1981.
2. For good critiques of the traditional leadership literature see *Leadership: Where Else Can We Go?* edited by Morgan W. McCall, Jr. and Michael M. Lombardo, Duke University Press, 1978, and the Leadership Symposium Series of books edited by James G. Hunt and Lars L. Larson, and published by the Southern Illinois University Press.
3. Cartoon by Stan Hunt.
4. See *Power in Management* by Kotter.
5. For more information on the situation, see "Zaphiropoulos" by John Kotter, HBS Case Services #9–480–044.
6. Lots of agreement seems to exist on this point. See, for example, "Two Words That are Hard to Say: You're Fired" by Bryant and Carole R. Cushing, *Wall Street Journal,* and "The Art of Firing an Executive" by Judson Gooding, *Fortune,* October 1972.
7. From *Fortune,* June 28, 1982, p. 91, "Managing by Mystique" by Myron Magnet.
8. See *The General Managers* by John Kotter.
9. See Tom Peters, "Symbols, Patterns, and Settings" in *Organizational Dynamics,* 1978.

10. See for example, "ITT: Can Profits be Programmed?" *Dun's Review*, November 1965.

11. See *Organization and Environment* by Paul Lawrence and Jay Lorsch, Harvard Business School, 1967.

12. See Peters, "Symbols, Patterns, and Settings."

13. From page 104, "The Unlikely Hero of McGraw-Hill" by Donald Holt, *Fortune*, May 21, 1979.

14. See "Choosing Strategies for Change" by John Kotter and Leonard A. Schlesinger, *Harvard Business Review*, March/April 1979.

15. See *A Theory of Leadership Effectiveness* by Fred E. Fiedler, McGraw-Hill, 1967, and *The General Managers* by Kotter.

Chapter 6

1. For a good detailed example of how a talented and successful young person can find himself having great difficulty with a boss, see "Tom Levick" by Gary Gerttula, HBS Case Services #9–480–049.

2. For a more detailed description of the situation, see First National City Bank Operating Group (A) and (B) by John Seeger, Jay Lorsch, and Cyrus Gibson, Case 7–1 in *Organization* by Kotter, Schlesinger, and Sathe, Irwin, 1979.

3. Names are described. This information comes from interviews with some of the people involved.

4. See, for example, John J. Gabarro, "Socialization at the Top: How CEOs and Their Subordinates Develop Interpersonal Contracts," *Organizational Dynamics*, Winter 1979; and John P. Kotter, *Power in Management*, AMACOM, 1979.

5. From the case "Frank Mason" by John J. Gabarro and N. J. Norman, HBS Case Services #6–476–019.

6. See Peter Drucker, *The Effective Executive*, Harper & Row, 1967.

Chapter 7

1. See Chapter 3 in *The General Managers* by John Kotter.

2. For more information on the method, see *Self-Assessment and*

Career Development by Kotter, Faux, and McArthur, Prentice-Hall, 1978.

3. For example, see Pfeffer's description on page 60 of *Power in Organizations* of how easily available indicators can be used to make judgments regarding the relative power of different functional departments within a business firm.

4. See Chapter 4 in *The General Managers* by Kotter.

5. Ed Banfield's work originally brought this pattern to my attention. Although he was talking about political figures in city government, the same seems to hold for very influential people in organizations generally. See *Political Influence*, The Free Press, 1961.

6. For a good discussion of this point, see G. Salancik and J. Pfeffer, "Who Gets Power—and How They Hold On to It: A Strategic Contingency Model of Power," *Organizational Dynamics*, Winter 1977.

7. See Chapter 3 in Kotter's *The General Managers*.

8. Simon & Schuster, 1976.

9. David McClelland has suggested, correctly I believe, that "America's concern about the possible misuse of power verges, at times, on a neurotic obsession." See "The Two Faces of Power," *Journal of International Affairs*, 1970, Vol. 24, No. 1, p. 44.

10. Henry Greenwald, the editor-in-chief of Time, Inc., has been quoted as saying something similar (see the February 1982 issue of *Cosmopolitan*. So has sociologist Rosabeth Kanter (see *Men and Women of the Corporation*, Basic Books, 1967).

Chapter 8

1. See Kotter's *The General Managers*, especially Chapter 2.

2. See, "How New York Bank Got Itself Entangled in Drysdale's Dealings" by Julie Salamon, *Wall Street Journal*, Friday, June 11, 1982, p. 1, and "Costly Caper" in *Time*, February 20, 1984, p. 61.

3. See *Decision Making at the Top* by Gordon Donaldson and Jay Lorsch.

4. For more details see "Parker Brothers" by Stengrevics and Kotter, HBS Case Services #9-480-047, and "Firm Plays it Safe

with Voluntary Recall" by Larry Kramer, *The Washington Post*, June 7, 1979.

5. For a good description of the Rely case see, "Taking Rely Off Market Cost Procter & Gamble a Week of Agonizing" by Dean Rotbart and John Prestbo, *Wall Street Journal*, November 3, 1980, p. 1.

6. The actual title is "How Moral Men Make Immoral Decisions," from *On A Clear Day You Can See General Motors* by J. Patrick Wright, Write Enterprises, Grosse Point, Michigan, 1979.

7. See *On A Clear Day You Can See General Motors* by Wright.

8. See pages 142 and 143 in Kotter's *The General Managers*.

9. Facts from "Roy Ash Is Having Fun at Addressogrief-Multigrief" by Louis Kraar, *Fortune*, February 27, 1978, pp. 47–52, and "AM International: When Technology Was Not Enough," *Business Week*, January 25, 1982, pp. 62–68.

10. See Chapter 3 in Kotter's *The General Managers*.

11. See, for example, Rumelt's *Strategy, Structure, and Economic Performance*, Harvard Business School, 1974.

12. Facts are from, "RCA: Still Another Master," *Business Week*, August 17, 1981, pp. 80–86, and RCA annual reports.

13. See "Choosing Strategies for Change" by Kotter and Schlesinger.

14. Facts from, "Federal Radar Corporation" by L. Wallace Clausen, Alfred G. Zappola, and J. Sterling Livingston, Peat, Marwick, Livingston, 1965.

15. For more details see Case 7–3 in *Organization* by Kotter, Schlesinger, and Sathe.

16. A Yankelovich, Skelly, and White survey in 1968 found that 70 percent of those polled agreed that "business tries to strike a fair balance between profits and interests of the public." When they asked the same question in 1977, only 15 percent agreed with the statement. As reported in *Business Week*, May 14, 1979.

Chapter 9

1. The facts in this case come from three primary sources:
    a. CBS: When Being No. 1 Isn't Enough," *Business Week*, May 26, 1980, pp. 128–132.

b. "Paley's Dismissal of Backe as CBS Chief Raises Question About Concern's Course" by John E. Cooney, *Wall Street Journal,* May 13, 1980, p. 48.
c. "CBS Names Wyman of Pillsbury to Replace Backe as the President" by John E. Cooney and Lawrence Ingrassia, *Wall Street Journal,* May 23, 1980, p. 2.
2. From "Top Executives Find the Going is Toughest When It's Time to Go," *Wall Street Journal,* August 21, 1980, p. 1.
3. See "Ford After Henry II," in *Business Week,* April 30, 1979, pp. 62–72. And "Dearborn Beckons: The Return of Henry Ford II," in *Fortune,* March 22, 1982.
4. The facts here come from "Why Harold Geneen got the Board to Strip Power from Hamilton" by Priscilla S. Meyer, *Wall Street Journal,* July 18, 1979, p. 1. And "ITT: Groping for a New Strategy," *Business Week,* December 15, 1980, pp. 66–80.
5. From "Limiting a CEO's Tenure," in *Dun's Business Month,* January 1982, page 68.
6. Facts from "Following the Corporate Legend," *Business Week,* February 11, 1980, pp. 65, 66.
7. From "Retirement as the Pinnacle of Your Career" by Mortimer R. Feinberg and Aaron Levenstein, a Manager's Journal feature in the *Wall Street Journal,* November 23, 1981.

Chapter 10

1. The specifics here and on the next few pages come from *History of the American Economy,* 3rd edition, by Ross N. Robertson, Harcourt Brace, Jovanovich, 1955, and "Rise and Evolution of Big Business" by Alfred D. Chandler, Jr. in *Encyclopedia of American Economic History* edited by Glenn Porter, Charles Scribner's Sons, 1980.
2. See "Rise and Evolution of Big Business" by Chandler.
3. For an excellent report on the rise of the modern business organization, see Alfred Chandler's *The Visible Hand* and *Strategy & Structure.*
4. For a further discussion of this Japan–USA comparison and its consequences, see Richard Pascale and Anthony Athos, *The Art of Japanese Management,* Simon and Schuster, 1981, especially Chapter 5.

Acknowledgments

1. The full report of this project was published as *Mayors in Action* by John P. Kotter and Paul R. Lawrence, John Wiley, 1974.

2. I am thinking of the Contingency Theory ideas articulated in *Organization and Environment* by Lawrence and Lorsch, Harvard Business School, 1967.

3. The work subsequently led to a book entitled *Organizational Dynamics,* by John Kotter Addison-Wesley, 1978.

4. This was published by AMACOM, in 1979, as *Power for Management* by John Kotter.

5. See, for example, Chapter 7 in *Organization* by Kotter, Schlesinger, and Sathe, Irwin, 1979.

6. Schein had been working in this area for a number of years. I helped on a study funded by the Carnegie Commission on Higher Education and did a small project of my own (a summary of the latter is reported as "The Psychological Contract: Managing the Joining Up Process," *California Management Review,* 1973, Vol. 15, No. 3, pp. 91–99).

7. This work was subsequently published by Prentice-Hall in 1978 as *Self-Assessment and Career Development* by Kotter, Faux, and McArthur.

8. None of the data from the project has been published as of 1982. But a conceptual overview of the project by Sonnenfeld and Kotter, came out in *Human Relations* under the title, "The Maturation of Career Theory."

9. The complete report of the project can be found in *The General Managers* by Kotter, Free Press, 1982.

10. This idea was originally brought to my attention by Wickham C. Skinner and Earl Sasser.

11. See *Political Influence* by Edward C. Banfield, Free Press, 1961; *Exchange and Power in Social Life* by Peter M. Blau, John Wiley, 1964; "Power Dependence Relations" by Richard M. Emerson, *American Sociological Review,* Vol. 27, No. 1 (February 1962); *Who Governs* by Robert A. Dahl, Yale, 1961; *Power: The Inner Experience* by David C. McClelland, Irvington Publishers, 1975; *Presidential Power* by Richard E. Neustadt, John Wiley, 1960.

BIBLIOGRAPHY

Across the Board. "Firing at the Top," October 1981, pp. 17–18.

ALLEN, ROBERT W.; MADISON, DAN L.; PORTER, LYMAN W.; REN-WICK, PATRICIA A.; and MAYES, BRONSTON T., "Organizational Politics; Tactics and Characteristics of Its Actors," *California Management Review,* Fall 1979, Vol. 22, No. 4, pp. 77–83.

BANFIELD, EDWARD C., *Political Influence.* New York: The Free Press, 1961.

BASS, BERNARD. *Stogdill's Handbook of Leadership.* New York: The Free Press, 1981.

BLAU, PETER M. *Exchange and Power in Social Life.* New York: John Wiley and Sons, Inc., 1964.

BOYATZIS, RICHARD. *The Competent Manager.* New York: John Wiley, 1982.

BREARLEY, A. "The Changing Role of the Chief Executive." *Journal of General Management,* to 1976, 3 (4), pp. 62–71.

Business Week. "CBS: When Being No. 1 Isn't Enough," May 26, 1980, pp. 128–132.

———. "Following the Corporate Legend," February 11, 1980, pp. 65–66.

———. "AM International: When Technology Was Not Enough," January 25, 1982, pp. 62–68.

———. "Ford After Henry II," April 30, 1979, pp. 62–72.

———. "ITT: Groping for a New Strategy," December 15, 1980, pp. 66–80.

———. "Still Another Master," August 17, 1981, pp. 80–86.

———. "When A New Product Strategy Wasn't Enough," February 18, 1980.

Chandler, Alfred D., Jr. "Rise and Evolution of Big Business," in *Encyclopedia of American Economic History.* New York: Charles Scribner's Sons, 1980.

———. *Strategy and Structure.* Cambridge, Mass.: MIT Press, 1962.

———. *The Visible Hand.* Cambridge, MA: Harvard University Press, 1977.

Clausen, L. Wallace; Zappola, Alfred G.; and Livingston, J. Sterling. "Federal Radar Corporation," Peat, Marwick, Livingston, 1965.

Cooney, John E. "Paley's Dismissal of Backe as CBS Chief Raises Question About Concern's Course." *Wall Street Journal,* May 13, 1980, p. 48.

Cooney, John E. and Ingrassia, Lawrence. "CBS Names Wyman of Pillsbury to Replace Backe as the President." *Wall Street Journal,* May 23, 1980, p. 2.

Cushing, Bryant and Carole R., "Two Words That Are Hard To Say: You're Fired," *Wall Street Journal.*

Dahl, Robert A. *Who Governs?* New Haven: Yale University Press, 1961.

Dalton, Melville. *Men Who Manage.* New York: John Wiley, 1959.

Donaldson, Gordon, and Jay Lorsch. *Decision Making at the Top.* New York: Banc Books, 1983.

Drucker, Peter. *Management.* New York: Harper & Row, 1974.

———. *The Effective Executive.* New York: Harper & Row, 1967.

Dun's Business Month. "Limiting a CEO's Tenure," January 1, 1982, p. 82.

Dun's Review, "ITT: Can Profits Be Programmed?". November 1965.

EMERSON, RICHARD M. "Power Dependence Relations." *American Sociological Review,* February 1962, Vol. 27, No. 1., pp. 31–41.

FEINBERG, MORTIMER R. and LEVENSTEIN, AARON. "Retirement as the Pinnacle of Your Career." Manager's Journal Feature, *Wall Street Journal,* November 23, 1981, p. 26.

FIEDLER, FRED E. *A Theory of Leadership Effectiveness,* New York: McGraw-Hill, 1967.

Forbes. "Is There Life After Downfall." November 2, 1979, pp. 241–250.

Fortune. "Dearborn Beckons: The Return of Henry Ford II," March 22, 1982, p. 13.

GABARRO, JOHN J. "Socialization at the Top: How CEOs and Their Subordinates Develop Interpersonal Contracts." *Organizational Dynamics,* Winter 1979.

——— AND KOTTER, JOHN P. "Managing Your Boss." *Harvard Business Review,* January/February 1980, pp. 92–106.

——— AND NORMAN, N.J. "Frank Mason." HBS Case Services #6-476-019.

GERTTULA, GARY A. "Tom Levick." HBS Case Services #9-480-049.

GOODING, JUDSON. "The Art of Firing an Executive," *Fortune,* October 1972.

HOLT, DONALD D. "The Unlikely Hero of McGraw-Hill." *Fortune,* May 21, 1979, pp. 97–108.

KANTER, ROSABETH. *Men and Women of the Corporation.* New York: Basic Books, 1977.

———. *The Change Masters.* New York: Simon and Schuster, 1984.

KOLB, DAVID A., RUBIN, IRWIN M., and MCINTYRE, JAMES M. *Organizational Psychology: A Book of Readings.* Englewood Cliffs, NJ: Prentice-Hall, Inc., 1979.

KOTTER, JOHN P. "Fred Henderson." HBS Case Services #9-480-043.

———. "MANAGING EXTERNAL DEPENDENCE." *Academy of Management Review 1979,* 1979, Vol. 4, No. 1, pp. 87–92.

———. *Organizational Dynamics: Diagnosis and Intervention.* Reading, MA: Addison-Wesley, 1978.

———. "POWER, DEPENDENCE, AND EFFECTIVE MANAGEMENT." *Harvard Business Review,* July/August 1977. pp. 125–136.

——. *Power In Management.* AMACOM, 1979.

——. "RENN ZAPHIROPOULOS." HBS CASE SERVICES #9-480-044.

——. *The General Managers.* New York: The Free Press, 1982.

——. "THE PSYCHOLOGICAL CONTRACT: MANAGING THE JOINING UP PROCESS." *California Management Review,* 1973, Vol. 15, No. 3, pp. 91-99.

——; FAUX, VICTOR A.; and MCARTHUR, CHARLES C. *Self-Assessment and Career Development.* Englewood Cliffs, NJ: Prentice-Hall, Inc., 1979.

KOTTER, JOHN P. and PAUL LAWRENCE, *Mayors in Action,* New York: John Wiley, 1974.

——, AND SCHLESINGER, LEONARD A. "Choosing Strategies for Change." *Harvard Business Review,* July/August 1979, pp. 106-114.

——; Schlesinger, Leonard A.; and SATHE, VIJAY. *Organization.* Homewood, IL: Richard D. Irwin, Inc., 1979.

KRAAR, LOUIS. "AM International: When Technology Was not Enough." *Business Week,* June 25, 1982, pp. 62-68.

——. "Roy Ash is Having Fun at Addressogrief-Multigrief." *Fortune,* February 27, 1978, pp. 47-52.

KRAMER, LARRY. "Firm Plays It Safe with Voluntary Recall." *Washington Post,* June 7, 1979.

LANGLEY, MONICA, "ATT Marketing Men Find Their Star Fails to Ascend as Expected," *Wall Street Journal,* February 13, 1984, page 1.

LAWRENCE, PAUL, AND LORSCH, JAY, *Organization and Environment.* Boston: Harvard University Press, 1967.

LEMANN, NICHOLAS. "The Split: A True Story of Washington Lawyers." *Washington Post,* March 23, 1980.

LORSCH, JAY and ALLEN, STEVEN A. *Managing Diversity and Interdependence.* Cambridge, MA: Harvard University Press, 1973.

MACCOBY, MICHAEL, *The Gamesman,* New York: Simon and Schuster, 1976.

MAGNET, MYRON. "Managing by Mystique at Tandem Computers." *Fortune,* June 28, 1982.

MCCALL, MORGAN W., JR. and LOMBARDO, MICHAEL. eds. *Leadership: Where Can We Go?* Durham, NC: Duke University Press, 1978.

McCLELLAND, DAVID C. *Power: The Inner Experience.* New York: Irvington Publishers, 1975.

―――. "The Two Faces of Power." *Journal of International Affairs,* 1970, Vol. 24, No. 1, pp. 29–47.

MEYER, HERBERT E. "Shootout at the Johns-Manville Corral." *Fortune,* October 1976, pp. 146–154.

MEYER, PRISCILLA S. "Why Harold Geneen Got the Board to Strip Power from Hamilton." *Wall Street Journal,* July 18, 1979, p. 1.

MILES, ROBERT H. *Macro Organizational Behavior.* Santa Monica, CA: Goodyear Publishing, 1980.

MORRISON, ANN. "CEO's Pick the Best CEO's." *Fortune,* May 4, 1981, pp. 133–135.

NEUSTADT, RICHARD E. *Presidential Power: The Politics of Leadership.* New York: John Wiley & Sons, Inc., 1960.

PASCALE, RICHARD T. and ATHOS, ANTHONY G. *The Art of Japanese Management.* Simon and Schuster, 1981.

PETERS, TOM. "Symbols, Patterns, and Settings." *Organizational Dynamics,* Fall 1978, pp. 3–23.

PETTIGREW, ANDREW. *The Politics of Organizational Decision Making.* London: Tavistock, 1973.

PFEFFER, JEFFREY. *Power in Organizations.* Marshfield, MA: Pitman Publishing, 1981.

PRESTHUS, ROBERT. *The Organizational Society.* New York: Vintage Books, 1962.

REICH, CHARLES. *The Greening of America.* New York: Random House, 1970.

ROBERTSON, ROSS N. *History of the American Economy.* 3rd ed., New York: Harcourt Brace Jovanovich, 1955.

ROTBART, DEAN and PRESTBO, JOHN A. "Taking Rely Off Market Cost Procter & Gamble a Week of Agonizing." *Wall Street Journal,* November 3, 1980, p. 1.

ROWAN, ROY. "ABC Covers Itself." *Fortune,* November 17, 1980.

RUMELT, RICHARD P. *Strategy, Structure, and Economic Performance.* Cambridge MA: Harvard University Press, 1974.

SALAMON, JULIE. "How New York Bank Got Itself Entangled in Drysdale's Dealings." *Wall Street Journal,* June 11, 1982, p. 1.

SALANCIK, G. and PFEFFER, J. "Who Gets Power And How They Hold On To It: A Strategic Contingency Model of Power." *Organizational Dynamics,* Winter 1977, pp. 3–21.

SAYLES, LEONARD. *Managerial Behavior.* New York: McGraw-Hill, 1964.

SCOTT, WILLIAM G. and HART, DAVID K. *Organizational America.* Boston: Houghton Mifflin, 1979.

SONNENFELD, JEFFREY and KOTTER, JOHN P. "The Maturation of Career Theory." *Human Relations,* 1982. Vol. 35, No. 1, pp. 19–46.

STENGREVICS, JOHN and KOTTER, JOHN P. "Fred Fischer," HBS Case Services #9–480–045.

———. "PARKER BROTHERS," HBS CASE SERVICES #9–480–047.

STEWART, ROSEMARY. *Contrasts In Management.* New York: McGraw-Hill, 1976.

Time. "Costly Caper," February 20, 1984, p. 61.

U.S. BUREAU OF THE CENSUS. *Statistical Abstract of the United States 1981,* Washington, DC: 1981, p. 142.

WRIGHT, J. PATRICK, *On a Clear Day You Can See General Motors.* Grosse Pointe, Michigan: Wright Enterprises, 1979.

INDEX